FINANCIAL LITERACY for Kids

FUN STORIES AND SMART LESSONS

to Teach Children How to Earn, Save, Spend, and Invest Money—Build Lifelong Skills Through Tips, Activities, and Games

LUCAS STERLING

TOP TIER PRESS

Published under the author brand **Lucas Sterling**

CONTENTS

NANCIAL

LITERACY

for Ki

INTRODUCTION

Hi there! I'm so glad you opened this book, because you're about to start a money adventure unlike any other. Have you ever held a shiny coin in your hand and wondered where it came from or what you could do with it? Maybe you've counted some bills in your piggy bank or tried to figure out how many weeks of chores it would take to save for that wonderful toy or cool new game. Or maybe you just think money is something grown-ups talk about while you'd rather be playing outside. No matter how you feel about it right now, trust me: Money isn't just for adults. Money is for everyone, including you!

Imagine if money was magic. This is not the wave-a-wand-and-poof kind of magic, but real-life magic. Something that lets you buy your favorite ice cream on a hot day, treat your best friend to a surprise snack, or even help someone who needs a little extra kindness. Pretty cool, right? In this book, we'll explore all the secrets of money together, and I promise you'll have lots of fun along the way. You won't just read boring rules or lists. Instead, you'll play games, solve puzzles, meet kids like you facing real money challenges, and try out hands-on activities to become your very own Money Master.

Why is learning about money important? Well, consider money to be a tool. Just like a superhero has special gear (like a cape or a gadget belt), understanding money gives you super skills for life. Whether you want to start your own mini-business, save up for something special, give to people or animals who need help, or feel confident each time you spend or save, knowing how money works is the key.

You might already know a few things about money, like where your allowance comes from or how much your favorite treat costs. But did you know that being smart with money can actually make things more fun and less stressful? A financial plan helps you reach your goals faster and ensures you have money when you need it. Plus, you might even discover creative ways to earn money, save it up for bigger dreams, and use it to bring a smile to someone's face.

But don't worry—you don't have to do this alone. All throughout this book, you'll meet kids just like you. Some love collecting coins, others are saving for a big dream, and some are figuring out the best way to share their money to make a difference. You'll hear their stories, cheer them on, and learn tricks they use to handle tricky situations, like choosing between spending and saving or earning money from doing helpful things around the house or neighborhood.

Are you ready to dive into awesome stories? Get your pencil ready for doodling ideas, playing games, and solving mini-mysteries about money. We'll visit places like markets, lemonade stands, and even invent our shops. You can choose what to buy, save for, and how to grow your money.

And here's the best part: there are no boring lectures here, just fun, interactive adventures. You'll get to answer questions about what you'd do in different situations (would you buy a comic book now or save for that skateboard later?), complete money missions, and even draw or write about your dream job or business idea. The goal isn't to tell you what to do but to help you think, imagine, and find your path to becoming smarter with money.

Maybe you're already dreaming about starting a pet-walking business, or selling crafts you made at home, or baking cookies and sharing them with your friends. Or maybe you just want to know why some things cost more than others, why it's important to save, or how banks work. This book will help you with all of that and show you how money goes far beyond your wallet or piggy bank.

You don't have to be good at math to understand money, either. Sure, numbers are part of it, but so are creativity, kindness, and making beneficial choices. For example, you'll learn fun tricks for counting coins and bills, but also how to set exciting goals, ask great questions, and make decisions that fit you and your family. You'll see how every coin and dollar is a chance to learn something new, not just about spending, but about yourself, your friends, and your community.

If you enjoy drawing, you can sketch your dream store or design your ultimate savings jar. If you like storytelling, you'll love thinking up ways money can help heroes in everyday life. And if you like solving mysteries, you'll find plenty of puzzles and challenges sprinkled throughout these pages. There's even space for you to write your own "Money Adventures," so you can look back at how much you've learned!

Are you still curious about why it matters? Well, money touches almost everything we do. It can help us treat ourselves but also help others. It lets us plan fun trips, adopt a pet, get cool school supplies, and sometimes even surprises us with new opportunities. By learning about money now, even just a little at a time, you'll be ready for whatever awesome adventures come your way.

Learning about money doesn't mean giving up fun or feeling stressed. It means you get to make choices, feel proud of your plans, and say yes to cool things because YOU decided how to spend, save, and share. And guess what? Grown-ups aren't born knowing everything about money, either they had to learn just like you will.

So let's get started! Open your mind, grab your favorite pen or a pile of colored markers, and join me as we explore the world of money. By the end of this book, you'll have all kinds of new skills, ideas, and stories to share, but most importantly, you'll feel excited and confident about using money in smart, thoughtful, and generous ways.

Are you ready to become a Money Master? Turn the page, and let's begin your adventure!

UNLOCK YOUR MONEY ADVENTURE JOURNAL

Ready to make learning about money fun, empowering, and practical?

As a thank-you for reading this book, I've created something special just for you: **The Money Adventure Journal.** This no-fluff guide is packed with fun challenges, smart trackers, and reflection pages that help you earn, save, and spend like a money pro. It's your space to dream big, plan smart, and build confidence with every dollar you make.

Inside your journal, you'll find:

- Cool activities and real-life money missions
- Trackers to help you save, spend, and share wisely
- Fun pages for setting goals and celebrating wins
- Simple tips to grow your money skills and confidence

Access Your Companion Workbook

Visit: **https://content.toptierpress.com/free-money-adventure-journal**

Or scan the QR code below to get instant access!

CHAPTER 1

WHAT IS MONEY, AND WHY IS IT IMPORTANT?

Imagine you're on the playground with your favorite snacks or toys, *hoping to trade with friends for something new and exciting.* But what happens when no one wants what you have? Or when someone wants to trade, but you don't quite like their offer? Trading can be tricky, right? Occasionally it's easy to swap things; other times it feels like a puzzle that's hard to solve. Have you ever stopped to wonder how people figured out a better way to share and exchange things so everyone could get what they wanted? What if there was *something special that made trading simple and fair for everyone*, something almost like magic that everyone could use? You're about to take a fun journey into the story behind those questions and discover how the idea of money came to help us all trade, save, and spend in ways that make life easier and more exciting.

Bartering and the Need for Money

The sun was shining when Jayden and Mia headed outside for recess with their classmates. Jayden looked at the bag of crunchy pretzels in his hand, his favorite snack, and wondered if anyone wanted to trade. Mia peeked into her backpack and smiled. She found her sparkly blue bouncy ball and thought, *"Maybe someone wants this."*

As soon as they reached the blacktop, Jayden grinned, *"Hey, Mia! That's a cool bouncy ball. Want to trade for some pretzels?"* Mia squeezed the ball and shook her head. *"Hmm, I love pretzels, but this bouncy ball bounces so high! I want to keep it."* Jayden shrugged, but then Emma walked up holding two shiny stickers. She asked, *"Mia, I'll trade you both these stickers for your bouncy ball!"* Mia's eyes lit up, she loved stickers. In a quick swap, Mia gave up her bouncy ball and got the stickers. Emma skipped away, tossing the bouncy ball and smiling.

Jayden watched the whole thing. He decided to offer his pretzels to Emma for a turn with the bouncy ball she just got. *"Can I give you all my pretzels for one bounce of your ball?"* Emma considered, but she shook her head. *"No thanks. I really like this ball!"* Jayden munched his pretzels and smiled, thinking about what trades he might try next time.

Trading like this is called **bartering.** When you barter, *you don't use money at all.* You swap things directly—one thing for another. Kids constantly do it without even knowing the word.

Here are some ways real kids might barter every day:

- Swapping a *soccer card* with a friend for a *shiny sticker*
- Giving half your *chocolate chip cookie* for someone's *juicy apple slice*

- Offering a *comic book* in exchange for a *cool action figure*
- Trading your *extra rubber dinosaur* for *three marbles* from your friend

For a barter to work, **both people** need to want what the other person has. They also have to feel the trade is **fair.** This sounds easy, but let's see what happens when things don't go smoothly.

During indoor spare time, Olivia showed off her fluffy pink eraser shaped like a cat. Alex wanted it, so he asked, *"Trade my green pencil for your eraser?"* Olivia frowned, *"No way! My old pencil's already green."* Just then, Noah walked by and offered a glitter pen instead, but Olivia still said no. *"Sorry, I want something else."* In this case, no one could agree. Even though everyone tried, nobody wanted what the others had. No trade happened at all.

Now picture five friends sitting in a circle, each holding different things: a bookmark, a pack of crayons, a racecar, a notebook, and a keychain. Imagine everyone wants something different. The girl with the crayons wants the notebook, but the notebook owner really wants the keychain. The keychain owner wants the bookmark, but the bookmark owner is looking at the crayons. The more people there are, the harder it gets to make trades everyone likes. Occasionally, no one can swap at all because the chain doesn't work out.

Try This: Schoolyard Swap

- Grab three friends and a few things to trade, like snacks, pencils, or toys.
- Take turns trying to make deals so everyone ends up with something they want.
- If someone doesn't want what's offered, the trade ends there.
- *How long can you keep trading before someone gets stuck?*

You might notice it works for a little while, but then trades slow down or stop completely!

Bartering also causes trouble over "saving up" trades. If someone says, *"Let me give you this drawing today, and you'll bring me a cookie tomorrow,"* there's a chance they might forget, change their mind, or just not want to do the trade later. Some kids might end up with nothing whatsoever. Without money, there's **no easy way** to keep track of *"half-finished"* trades.

Imagining a bigger playground, people would eventually want to trade with people they don't know or don't see every day. Let's say someone wants a mitten someone else has, but all they can offer is a toy dinosaur the mitten owner doesn't want. Suddenly, the trade just doesn't work! It gets confusing and slow. People get left out or feel frustrated if nobody wants what they're offering.

This makes you wonder: could there be *something everyone wants,* something people will always accept? What if there was a **special object** like tokens or shells that worked as a promise you could trade for anything you like? Wouldn't it be easier if people earned these special things for what they gave and spent them on whatever they wanted?

Trading without money can be fun, but it's messy and sometimes unfair. Kids everywhere started inventing ways to fix these trading puzzles. That's how the first people who lived long ago started thinking about money. Imagine a world where money didn't exist and the amazing ideas people came up with to solve the problem! The next adventure will show how money first came to be and how it helped people trade, save, and buy things everywhere.

The Invention and Types of Money

Imagine you want a red ball from your friend, but all you have is an apple to swap. What if your friend doesn't want an apple? Maybe he wants a pencil, but you don't have one. Bartering like this worked for a while. But after people started running into these problems again and again, they asked, *"What if there was something that everyone wanted, something you could trade for anything?"* That's how the idea for money appeared, like a clever trick that made life and trading easier for everyone.

Money became the solution. Instead of searching for exactly what the other person wanted every single time, you could just use money. If you had coins or special objects everyone trusted, you could trade them for anything, from sweet honey to warm bread. So if you wanted that red ball, but your friend only liked pencils, you didn't have to go looking for them first. You could just pay with money, and both of you would be happy.

Back in **ancient times,** people experimented with what could count as money. In some places along the beach, people used *shiny shells* because they were lovely and hard to find. In cold lands, *smooth stones* or *beads* served as money. On some islands, *huge round stones* were the most special money of all. In Africa and parts of Asia, long ago, people even traded with *salt,* because it kept their food fresh and everybody needed it. Later on, as ideas spread, money turned into little pieces of metal. These were gold, silver, and copper coins, each chosen for being valuable and tricky to copy. Then paper bills arrived. Picture someone holding their very first colorful paper bill, entirely different from a heavy metal coin. It's lighter, easy to fold, and small enough to hide in a shoe or tuck in a pocket.

Money didn't stop changing there. It grew up alongside people. Today, you use money for all sorts of cool things. When you go to the store with your mom or dad and help pay for groceries, you're using money. Maybe you get coins from your grandpa for cleaning your room, or you watch your older sister save bills in a piggy bank to buy a new book. Sometimes people use money to help others by donating to charity jars or fundraising for animal shelters. Money lets us share, save, spend, and plan for the future.

When you peek into a grown-up's wallet, you might find metal coins; some small and smooth, others big and thick. They have pictures pressed into them: faces of presidents, animals like eagles, or cool shapes and numbers showing how much they're worth. Paper bills look different too. They can be green, blue, or purple, depending on where you live. Some feel soft, others crisp, and sometimes they have see-through windows or shine under the light. Have you noticed some coins have holes in the center? Kids in Japan use coins with holes, and in Australia, bills are so bright and slippery, they're almost like little rainbows you can buy things with.

Try remembering a time at the store when someone used a plastic card instead of cash. These cards, called debit or credit cards, help pay for things by moving money electronically, almost like **invisible coins** racing through wires and bouncing into your bank account. Some money **isn't even something you can hold.** Have you ever used *game credits* on your tablet, *traded points in a phone app,* or watched your parents pay with their *smartphone?* That's **digital money,** and it can travel across oceans in one second, faster than any gold coin ever could.

Money all over the world wears different outfits. In England, the queen appears on coins. In Canada, there's a shiny coin called a *"loonie"* with a bird on it. In China, paper bills glow with magical *dragons* and towers. Once upon a time on a faraway island, people used round stones taller than your school desk as money; the bigger the stone, the richer you were! Everyone around them trusts each coin and bill, even though they may look different.

If you could invent your money, what would it look like? Perhaps a coin that is shaped like a star or a dinosaur. Maybe a bill that changes colors in the light, or a coin with your pet's smiling face on it, cool to the touch and fun to flip. Imagine money that smells sweet like strawberries or glows in the dark. *Dream up your designs because the story of money is always changing,* and someday you could help create the next new kind.

Creative Currency Design Activity

Earlier in this chapter, you explored what money looks like and how people use it. Now you get to design your very own version! Look around at the coins and bills you know. Every penny, nickel, or dollar bill holds its own world of color, numbers, and tiny details. Some have portraits of famous people, while others show wild animals, tall buildings, or shimmering statues. It's fun to think that every country, and sometimes even every state, likes to make its money look unique. Take a close look at a coin or bill from your wallet. What makes it stand out? Maybe it's the shiny edge, the large number in the middle, or the intricate pattern running around the side. Let those ideas swirl in your head as you get ready to become a money inventor.

Think like a real designer as you set out to create something new. This is your chance to dream up a coin or bill that only you could imagine, something that nobody else in the world owns. Your money can be any color you like. Bright green with blue stripes? Sure! Neon pink with silver dots? Why not! Money doesn't have to stick to gray or green. You get to decide how your new creation looks and feels.

Start with the shape and size. Will yours be a round coin the size of a cookie or a square bill as big as your hand? Try drawing a large circle, square, or even a star for your base. Grab crayons, pencils, markers, or anything else you'd like to use. Think about what will make your design stand out to anyone who sees it. Some real coins in the world have holes right through the middle. Others have unique edges that feel bumpy or smooth. Want to add a dotted border or put rainbow spots all along the outside? Go for it!

What would you put at the center? Maybe there's a picture or a little scene. You could draw a happy cat, a super-fast train, a rocket blasting to the moon, or even a pile of your favorite snacks. Your coin or bill can showcase animals, sports, silly faces, or magical creatures. You might want to sketch a sun with sunglasses, a dragon doing a dance, or your very own pet. Some people even make up pretend creatures or use funny symbols that mean something just to them.

Give your new money a name that shows off its personality. Try coming up with something that makes you smile or grabs attention right away. What about *"Giggly Coins," "Shiny Sparkle Bucks," or "Lightning Dollars"?* Maybe you think of *"Eco Tokens"* with a leafy plant or *"Star Power Credits"* with twinkling stars around a mega hero. Write your name somewhere on the money, either in big bubble letters or as a secret code that only your friends would understand.

Add a value somewhere on your design. Decide if your coin is worth 1, 5, or 10 of something, or invent your style of numbers. Maybe your bill is worth *"50 silvers"* or *"2 lucky points."* Try out different ways to show numbers. You can use large, bold fonts in the corners, fancy script in the middle, or even tiny numbers sprinkled around like confetti.

It's time for more details. Scatter stars or circles along the edges. Draw swirling lines, zigzags, hearts, or a row of tiny crowns. Get creative with patterns and borders. Add a small mark or stamp, maybe your initials or a tiny doodle, to make each piece unique. If you want to make your money extra special, cut it out of colorful paper, use stickers, or glue on shiny decorations. If you're designing on a computer or tablet, play with shapes and colors that look appealing together.

Think about what matters to you. People in different countries choose symbols that represent something special about their home. For example, Canada features beavers and maple leaves on its coins. In Australia, you might spot a kangaroo. Your money could show the street where you play, a favorite place, or even the name of your school or pet. If your brother or friend helped you, both of you could add ideas and work together as a money-making team.

"My friend Drew made a 'Dragon Dollar' with a picture of a friendly dragon and a shiny rainbow background. It was worth three giggles!" What story could your new money tell? Maybe yours is for trading laughs, sharing prizes, or starting your own pretend store.

The biggest rule is that there are no limits. Let your creativity go wild. Your coin or bill can be funny, bold, elegant, or all about something you love most. After you finish, celebrate what you've made! You've just joined the club of money inventors around the world.

Now that we've explored how bartering led to the invention of money and seen all the different shapes, colors, and stories money can have, you're ready to think like a true money inventor. Understanding why money was created helps us see how important it is for making trades fair, simple, and fun. With your own creative coin or bill design, you've taken a big step into the fascinating world of money, where ideas turn into something everyone can use. As you keep learning about saving, spending, and earning, remember that money isn't just coins and bills; it's a tool that connects people and helps us share what we have. Get ready for the next adventure, where you'll discover even more ways to make smart money choices and become a confident money master!

CHAPTER 2
HOW KIDS CAN EARN THEIR MONEY

Max's hands trembled as he counted the few coins he had earned that afternoon. It wasn't a gift or allowance from his parents; it was money he had worked for himself. But starting out wasn't easy. His stomach twisted at the thought of conversing with strangers, as he wondered if anyone would even stop at his wobbly lemonade stand. Across the street, neighbors seemed busy, and Max worried that his effort might go unnoticed. The small sign he'd made looked bright, but would it be enough to catch someone's eye? As the sun dipped lower, the first customer appeared, and Max took a deep breath, ready to greet them with a smile.

Many kids feel this mix of excitement and nervousness when they try something new, especially when it comes to earning money on their own. It's not just about the coins or bills; it's about learning to take chances, solve problems, and see what happens when you turn an idea into action. Occasionally the hardest part is figuring out where to start or understanding the difference between being given money and working to earn it.

This journey can teach kids skills that last a lifetime while showing them what responsibility and creativity truly mean.

Starting Your Small Business: Lemonade Stands and Beyond

Max stood at the end of his driveway, a wrinkled dollar bill pinched between his fingers. A neighbor had just bought lemonade from the wobbly stand he built out of an old box. His heart pounded with excitement. This dollar didn't come from his birthday card or a gift from his grandma. Max had squeezed lemons, mixed sugar, made a big sign with his favorite marker, and called out to everyone who walked by. Holding the dollar, he felt like a real entrepreneur.

Earning money feels exciting because you are the one making it happen. It's much more than just getting coins from your parents or surprise bills in your envelope. When you earn it, every shiny coin tells a story of effort, ideas, and a little bit of bravery.

Kids can earn money by starting their own small businesses. Although it may seem like only adults engage in it, child-run businesses exist in a variety of forms. Think about classic lemonade stands, handmade crafts, or even simple chores for a neighbor. All you need is an idea and a bit of courage. Imagine you and your friend are chatting at a café. One of you says, "What if we make friendship bracelets and sell them after school?" Soon you're listing what you'd need: lots of colorful string, maybe some beads, little bags for wrapping, and a bright sign to catch people's eyes. Starting out, you might need help. That's where parents come in. They can help you find supplies and help you set up somewhere safe, like your front yard or that busy corner at the playground.

Think about selling cookies. First, you need to pick a recipe. You'll need flour, sugar, eggs, and maybe your favorite chocolate chips. Next, you ask someone at home to help with the oven. When the warm cookies come out, you wrap them and set up a small table. To get people to notice, you make a colorful sign using your brightest markers and maybe add a drawing of a smiling cookie. If you want, you can even make up a catchy jingle to sing: "Yummy cookies here, baked fresh just for you!" Adding a special touch makes everything you sell stand out.

What helps a business do well? Creativity and effort. Drawing fun pictures or doodles on your signs makes people smile. Sometimes, wearing a silly hat or costume gets attention. Maybe you think of funny names for your cookies, like "Superpower Chocolate Chip" or "Magic Rainbow Sugar." Your effort shows when you give a big grin with each sale or decorate your stand with colorful balloons.

Running a business includes several simple steps that can be remembered easily:

1. Think of your idea. What do you enjoy doing or making?
2. Make a plan. What will you sell or do? What supplies do you need?
3. Gather supplies with the help of someone at home.
4. Find the right spot or people to visit. Perhaps it's your sidewalk, your neighbor's yard, or your school fair.

5. Tell people about your shop. Signs, songs, or even asking your parents to tell friends helps.
6. Ask for help when you need it. Adults can help with safety, money, or making sure your plan works.
7. Check your prices and count your money after you're done.

Sometimes it's tricky to talk to people you don't know or decide how much to charge. That's okay. Start by practicing what you'll say. You can even stand in front of your family and pretend they're new customers. If you're unsure about prices, look up what things cost at local stores or ask your parents for advice.

Earning money from a business is not the same as getting an allowance. An allowance is money you receive for being you or for helping around the house. Maybe you walk the dog or set the table, and you get a few dollars each week. But when you rake leaves for a neighbor or run a lemonade stand, you're trading your hard work and creativity for cash. Both feel good, but earning makes you even prouder. You solved a problem or made something helpful, and that means every dollar feels like a little trophy.

There's a story about Mia, who made colorful bookmarks using recycled paper and markers. She was nervous the first day and only sold one. But she didn't give up. The next day, she added glitter and drew tiny animals on each bookmark. Soon, her friends lined up to buy their favorites. Mia grinned all day. She had started with a tiny idea and turned it into her very own way to earn money.

Every time you earn, you're learning. You get better at talking to people, handling coins and bills, and making choices about what to do next. You discover what works and what doesn't. Most of all, you feel confident and proud because you made something real happen.

There are so many ways to earn money. You might do jobs around your house, help neighbors with their pets, or lend a hand to family friends. The world is full of little jobs for smart, creative kids who aren't afraid to ask, "How can I help?" There's always another adventure waiting to be discovered.

Easy Ways to Earn Money at Home or in Your Neighborhood

When a child wants to earn money, the first place to look is often close to home. Many jobs for young people start right in their neighborhood. For example, simple household chores in someone else's home can be a great beginning. Tasks like watering the flower pots on Mrs. Carter's porch or sweeping the walkway for the Sanchez family help others while giving you a chance to earn money. These jobs don't need much equipment, though a watering can or broom might come in handy. After asking politely if extra help is needed, a child might say, "I can water your plants on Mondays and Thursdays while you're at work. Would that be helpful for you?" People appreciate when someone takes care of their space, and being respectful makes it easier to get started.

Some kids love animals and can offer to walk a friendly dog for a neighbor or care for a pet when its owner is away. Scott, age ten, noticed Mr. Patel's dog barking in the backyard and asked, "I can walk Max around the block when you're busy. Should I bring my own leash, or does Max have a favorite one?" Pet jobs teach responsibility and build trust because animals rely on being fed and cared for on time. A trusted helper keeps a list of things to do, such as checking the water bowl or letting parents know when walking alone isn't safe. Kids can learn pet safety tips from family members, neighbors, or by reading brochures at the local animal shelter.

In many neighborhoods, raking leaves or picking up sticks offers a chance to work outdoors and care for the community. A sturdy rake or a pair of gloves makes the job easier. Once, Maya and her younger brother teamed up to clean Mr. Greenberg's yard. They worked quickly, filled bags to the top, and stacked them neatly at the curb. Mr. Greenberg smiled and said, "You both made my yard look great! Will you come back after the wind blows again?" Taking on a job with friends or siblings makes it more fun, and dividing the pay teaches fairness and teamwork.

Washing cars or bicycles is another job that brings quick results. Soap, buckets, sponges, and soft cloths are all you need. Neighbors might welcome someone careful and thorough to keep their cars shining. Before starting, kids can ask, "Would you like me to clean the outside only, or do you want the inside vacuumed too?" Working step by step shows good attention to detail. Always check with an adult before using supplies since everyone likes their things treated with care.

Sending a text, helping an older neighbor use a new TV remote, or showing a grandparent how to make a video call can feel like magic to someone who struggles with technology. Young people often learn about gadgets in school or through play. If you're good with electronics, offer politely: "I know how to set up email on a tablet. Would you like me to show you?" Speak slowly, be patient, and listen carefully. Sometimes a small bit of help opens the door for someone to enjoy music, talk to family, or play new games. That can feel even better than earning money.

Staying responsible from start to finish makes any small job a big deal. People remember when their helper arrives on time, does the work properly, and doesn't quit early. Being trusted means cleaning up after the job, putting away tools, and saying thank you at the end. Responsible helpers also speak kindly and honestly. If something goes wrong, tell the adult right away. Saying, "I couldn't reach the top shelf, so I left the plants on the counter for you," sounds thoughtful and respectful. When you finish a job just as promised, adults are more likely to call you again or tell their friends that you're reliable.

Here's how earning money brings more than just cash. Every new job builds courage and teaches valuable skills, such as keeping track of time, talking to new people, and solving small problems. Each time you help someone or complete a task, you feel proud of what you've learned. Even discovering that some jobs aren't your favorite helps you understand yourself better. These first steps open the door to bigger opportunities later.

Look around the homes and yards on your street or in your building. Notice what needs to be done, and practice asking, "Would it help if I helped with…?" Choose one job you could try this week. Write down what you'll need and who you'll talk to first. This simple plan moves you toward real money-earning adventures by taking action right where you live.

Make Your Own Money-Making Plan: A Weekly Activity

Anyone can make a plan to earn money, regardless of their skills or interests. That means you, too! Some kids like to draw and might sell bookmarks or cards they make. Others may be adept at taking care of pets, like walking Mrs. Garcia's dog after school. Maybe you notice a neighbor who always has leaves in her yard and could use some help raking them up, or a parent who'd love someone to organize the bookshelf for a small reward. You can help others and make money in many ways. You've already learned how to watch for opportunities, talk to adults, and show you can be responsible. These are the building blocks for making your own money-making plan.

Now it's time to put your ideas into action. This is about making your very own "My Money-Making Plan" that you can start using this week. Here's how you do it, step by step. First, get a piece of paper or open a special notebook. Make this your planning space. For Step 1, write down three ideas for ways you could earn money over the next week. These can be simple jobs or creative projects. Some examples might be washing a neighbor's car, making and selling friendship bracelets, babysitting your little brother or sister while your parents finish chores, watering plants for someone on vacation, or baking cookies to sell at a family gathering.

Once you have your three ideas, move on to Step 2: write out what you'll need for each activity. If you want to wash cars, you might need soap, a bucket, big sponges, and towels. If you want to make bracelets, you might want colorful string or beads, scissors, and maybe a comfortable spot to work. If you plan to offer to babysit, your list might say games or puzzles, snacks (with permission), and a way to contact an adult if you need help. Be as clear as possible so you don't find yourself missing something important at the last second.

For Step 3, look at each idea and ask yourself how long it will take to finish. Will raking leaves fill your entire Saturday afternoon, or just an hour before dinner? Could making bracelets for your neighbor be done after homework, or do you need a few days to get enough ready? Note how long you think each task will take and when you want to do it. Try to be honest with yourself; if you already have lots of soccer practice, maybe babysitting is better for a day when you have more free time. Planning ahead like this isn't just helpful; it's what a real business owner does.

Step 4 is all about who you'll talk to about your idea. Write down the names of the people you need to ask; maybe it's your parents, so you're sure it's okay and safe. It might be your neighbor or your friend's family if you hope to work together. Practice what you'll say, such as, "I'd like to earn some money this week by helping out." Could I wash your car on Saturday?" or "Would you like to buy a bookmark I drew for one dollar?" The more ready you are, the easier it will be to share your plan.

Keep working on your plan this week, checking in with yourself each day to see how things are going. Near the end of the week, look at how your plan worked out. Ask yourself what was easy and what was tricky. Did washing the car take longer than you thought, or was making bracelets messier than you expected? Maybe you ran out of lemonade too fast or forgot to ask someone for permission until the last minute. These moments are for learning. If you decide to try again, you can allocate more time, prepare more lemonade beforehand, or seek assistance with setup. Learning to change your plan helps you get better at every new challenge, not just earning money.

Don't forget to cheer yourself on! Every dollar, quarter, or even just a smile from someone you helped is something to be proud of. Earning money with your ideas gives you skills and confidence you'll use all your life. Mistakes just show you're trying hard and getting stronger. In later chapters, you will be able to try other challenges that help you grow your skills and confidence, just like the money-making plan you are working on now.

Now that you've discovered how exciting and rewarding it can be to earn your money through creative ideas and helping others, you're ready to take the next step. Whether it's starting a lemonade stand, walking a neighbor's dog, or selling handmade crafts, every little job teaches you important skills like planning, responsibility, and confidence. Keep exploring new ways to use your talents, and don't be afraid to try again if something doesn't work the first time. With each effort, you're not just earning money; you're building your independence and learning how to make smart choices that will help you throughout your whole life. So grab your notebook, think of your next money-making plan, and get ready for even more fun adventures ahead!

CHAPTER 3

SAVING LIKE A SUPER SAVER

The first time Mia saw the sparkling new skateboard in the shop window, her eyes lit up with excitement. She reached into her pocket, hoping to find enough money from her allowance. But all she found were a few lonely coins, far from what she needed to bring that board home. It was easy to feel disappointed and wonder if saving up was even possible.

Every day afterward, Mia glanced at her little jar on the shelf, wondering if those small coins could ever add up to something big. She wrestled with the urge to spend what she had right away, but something inside told her to wait, to keep adding a coin here and there, even when it felt slow. Saving wasn't about having a lot all at once; it was about what you could do every day, step by step, toward your dream. What would it feel like to turn those tiny bits of money into a real reward, like a secret superpower waiting to be discovered?

The Superpower of Saving and the Story of the Piggy Bank

Imagine you spot the coolest remote-control car at the store. You can picture it zipping across your living room, doing loops, flips, and wild turns. You reach for your wallet or dig into your pocket, but all you find are a few crumpled dollars and some coins. That awesome car costs way more than what you have right now. It feels discouraging, but what if you could turn yourself into a super saver, like a hero with a secret power?

A little voice squeaks from your shelf. "Over here! It's me, Penny the piggy bank!" Penny wiggles her round tail, her snout shining and pink. "Lots of people think I'm just a place to drop loose change, but I know the secret to turning spare coins into big dreams." Penny glances at your handful of coins. "Every super saver starts small. That's how my own adventure began. Want to hear about it?"

"Once, a kid wanted a bright blue yo-yo that cost three dollars. He emptied his pockets and groaned when he saw a pile of eight pennies and a sticky old piece of candy. 'It's not enough!' he said. But I whispered back, 'It's plenty to begin!' Every evening after that, he checked for extra coins in the couch cushions, on the sidewalk, or near the washing machine. If he found a quarter, that went in me with a little plink. If it was just a penny, it went in anyway."

Penny's belly glows with excitement. "Let's see how this works. If you put just one quarter, a 25-cent coin, in me every day, how much money do you think you'll have after one week?" Penny does a little hop. "Multiplying seven days by twenty-five cents results in $1.75!" And if you keep going for four whole weeks, that's 28 days. Twenty-five cents times 28 is…" She pauses so you can add it up. "That's $7.00! Enough for a yo-yo and even a snack."

Penny remembers watching coins drop in one by one. Occasionally a nickel would slip through the slot; other days a shiny dime or a big, clunky quarter. "Each morning, I'd wake up hoping for a new jangly surprise. Some days we found a lot, some days only one coin. It didn't matter, because saving a little bit as often as you can is still saving. The important part is putting in something again and again."

A few times, the kid almost opened Penny up early to buy gum or a treat. "The urge was strong. Gum now or maybe wait for the yo-yo?" Penny tapped her side, remembering. "Every super saver faces moments like these. My job is to protect your coins and help you wait for the bigger reward. When we felt tempted, we thought about how fun that first yo-yo trick would be, and we decided to save a little longer."

Inside Penny, the pile grew higher and shinier. Pennies and nickels mixed with dimes and quarters. "Whenever we looked inside, we'd count and cheer, even if the next coin was just a penny. Watching the pile grow made us feel proud, like superheroes on a quest. Don't give up, super saver! Every tiny step matters." Penny beamed with pride, remembering the day she jingled and rattled with enough coins. "We danced in a circle when we finally got the yo-yo. It wasn't just the toy that felt great; it was knowing we did it, and we did it together using the saving superpower!"

Think about something you've wanted, like a soccer ball, art supplies, movie tickets, or a trip to the ice cream shop. Picture your own piggy bank or jar slowly filling up, day after day. What would it feel like to reach inside and celebrate when you achieve your goal? Penny asked, "What is your dream? What would you love to save for if you knew you had a super saver's superpower?"

Everyone can be a super saver, Penny promised. You don't have to start with a ton of money. You just need to save often and stay on track. If you ever feel stuck, remember that every coin brings you closer. Even if you miss a day, you can always keep going. The adventure is about trying, not being perfect.

Penny gave a final wiggle. "Real super savers always have a goal. When you know what you're reaching for, your savings grow faster, and every coin means more. Once you pick your dream, saving turns into a real-life adventure."

Setting Savings Goals That Make Dreams Come True

Remember when the piggy bank started filling up and it seemed like anything was possible, just by adding coins day after day? That feeling doesn't have to stop at the bank. The next step to becoming a super saver is giving your savings a mission. When your money has a purpose, every coin feels more exciting, and your dream doesn't seem so far away. Maybe you've noticed how grown-ups write lists or keep calendars to make their big ideas happen. You can use the same kind of plan for things that matter to you.

First, pick something you really want. It could be a skateboard, a movie night, or tickets to see your favorite animal at the zoo. Sometimes it's one special thing, but sometimes it's something fun to do with people you care about. The most important part is choosing something you'll look forward to. Picture how you'll feel when you finally get it. That's the dream you're setting your sights on.

Once your dream is clear, it's time to find out the price. If you're eyeing a craft kit at the store, check the tag. Want to save for a birthday outing? Ask an adult to help you look up the cost online. Write the number down; numbers are like secret codes to your goal. Knowing the cost turns the dream into something real you can work toward.

Now make your dream even sharper by picking a deadline. Decide when you'd like to have your new soccer ball or join your friends at the amusement park. Is there a special date coming up, like your next school break or someone's birthday? Pick a day and circle it on your calendar, or draw a little symbol so you can see it coming closer. Goals feel easier when you can picture how soon you'll get there.

Take a minute to count how much money you can save each week. This might be your allowance, money from chores, or, birthday gifts from family. Don't forget coins you find in the sofa or little bits from helping a neighbor. Every small amount adds up. For example, if you can save $2 each week, write it down next to your goal.

Now comes the fun part: see how your dream breaks into smaller steps. Divide the total cost by how much you can save each week. If you want a jigsaw puzzle that costs $24 and you can save $2 per week, you know it will take twelve weeks. Saving $3 a week for something that costs $18 gets you there in six weeks. Math helps you see the path clearly and keeps your goal within reach.

To make saving feel more fun and real, try drawing a chart. Each time you add money to your piggy bank, color in a space or add a sticker. Watching your chart fill up gets more exciting with every deposit you make. You could tape your chart on the wall or keep it in your notebook. Some kids use pictures; for example, draw a rocket and color a stripe every time you save, getting closer to blast-off. Progress trackers are like cheering for yourself every step of the way.

Tell a friend or someone in your family about your plan. Sharing your goal can make you feel proud and give you someone to celebrate with when you reach the finish line. They might have tips of their own or help you stay strong when you get the urge to spend early. You can even make a savings club and work on your goals together.

Sometimes it's challenging to wait. Other things will try to grab your attention, like snacks at the store or a small toy. Try some saving tricks: keep your jar or bank in a special place, only open it every two weeks, or ask an adult to hold onto it until you reach your goal. If you accidentally spend some of your savings, don't worry. Super savers always try again and learn from each step.

When you're saving for something real, it becomes more exciting to see your coins add up. One day you'll count and realize you're halfway there or even close to your goal. Every deposit brings you closer, and the chart makes every step feel like a little victory.

The secret to making saving even simpler comes from putting your money into teams. Soon, you'll learn how to sort your savings into different jars: one for saving, one for spending, and one for sharing. You might decorate these jars or boxes and use them to keep your plans organized and fun, setting up each dollar for action.

Make Your Own Save–Spend–Share Jars Activity

After planning your dreams and savings goals, it's time to bring your plans to life with something you can see and use every day. This activity uses simple jars, or whatever you have handy, to turn big wishes into real steps you can follow. Lily looked at her drawing of a shiny new bike from the last section and grinned, ready to try a new way to keep her money organized. Maybe you want to save for a board game, spend on ice cream with friends, or share with someone who needs a helping hand. These jars help make it happen, little by little.

Start by gathering three small containers. You might use clear jars left over from pasta sauce, plastic cups, or boxes from old board games. If you can't find any, grab a piece of paper and draw three large circles or rectangles. These will be your "jars" for today. Gather some markers, stickers, tape, or anything you want to decorate with.

Next, give each jar a name. Write "Save" on one jar, "Spend" on the next, and "Share" on the last. Try your neatest printing or bubble letters if you like shapes and colors. Add stickers of stars, smiley faces, or even a little drawing of what each jar means to you. Maybe your "Save" jar has a rocket ship for big dreams, your "Spend" jar is covered in bright lightning bolts, and your "Share" jar gets kind hearts. Your jars can be as simple or creative as your imagination allows.

The "Save" jar keeps your money safe for wishes that need time, like Lily's bike or special tickets to the zoo next summer. If you want to get something big, saving up in this jar adds up coin by coin. Maybe you drop in the five dollars grandma gave you for your birthday and watch it grow toward your goal. The "Spend" jar is for fun things you can enjoy soon, such as picking a snack after school or trying that new eraser at the store. You might put half of your weekly allowance here, ready for a reward after working hard. The "Share" jar holds money for helping others. Imagine giving to a classroom plant project, buying a card for a friend, or saving a few coins so your school can buy new books for everyone.

Take a minute to brainstorm what you'd like to put in each jar. Get your parent or a buddy to talk ideas through. Max wanted to save for skateboard wheels; he decided to put his "pet-sitting" earnings in both the "Save" and "Share" jars because helping out made him feel good, and giving a bit too felt right. Maybe you choose to add coins you find lying around to your "Spend" jar for a fun surprise when you open it next.

Once you have ideas, set up your jars in a special spot. The kitchen counter, your bedroom shelf, or even a corner of your desk works well. The point is to make it somewhere you'll see often. When allowance day comes, think about how you want to split any money you get. Some kids like to put the first coin in "Save," the next in "Spend," then "Share," and keep going in that order. Others make colorful pie charts or track every coin and bill in a special "Super Saver Log." If you want, grab a piece of paper and create your own chart. Draw three columns: one for "Save," one for "Spend," and one for "Share." Every time you add money, put a tally mark or a small drawing, like a dollar sign, to watch your jars filling up.

Decorating makes the jars even more fun. Caleb put a sticker of a comic book hero on his "Save" jar to remind him he's a "super saver" every time he drops in a coin. Sophia wrapped her "Share" jar in rainbow tape, saying it made her want to give even more for next week's school bake sale.

Every jar counts, no matter how little or much you put in. If you made your jars out of drawings or shoeboxes, they work just as well. The best part is watching your money add up over time. Every single time you drop something in a jar, you're making your plan come alive, step by step. When you finally pull out enough from your "Save" jar to reach your wish, or when you get to buy snacks with your "Spend" jar, or give a surprise to someone from your "Share" jar, you'll know you're a real super saver, ready for new dreams each time.

Now that you know how saving even small amounts can grow into big rewards and how setting clear goals makes your dreams feel closer, it's time to start your own super saver adventure. By using the save, spend, and share jars and keeping track of your progress, you'll see every coin bring you one step nearer to something special. Remember, saving is not about being perfect but about trying again and again, celebrating each little win along the way. So grab your piggy bank or jars, pick a goal that excites you, and watch how your saving superpower helps turn wishes into wonderful realities!

CHAPTER 4
SPENDING SMART (NOT SILLY!)

Did you know that many people spend their money without stopping to think about what they truly need versus what they just want? Sometimes, even grown-ups find it tricky to decide whether to buy something important or something fun. What if you had a simple way to figure out which things should come first when you spend your money? Imagine having the confidence to make choices that help you feel good now and later. Exploring how to tell the difference between needs and wants can be the key to spending smart, and enjoying every penny along the way.

Understanding Wants vs. Needs: Why It Matters

Imagine you have five shiny coins in your pocket. You pick them up and start to wonder: What should I do with this money? Before you spend, it helps to know the difference between things you must have and things that would just be nice to have. Lots of kids (and grown-ups too) use their money without thinking about this. That's why sorting out "needs" and "wants" is one of the first smart money tricks you can learn.

A "need" is anything you must have to live, stay safe, and be healthy. Think about waking up in the morning and getting ready for school. You might eat a bowl of oatmeal (food), fill your water bottle (water), and put on your favorite jacket (clothes). These are all examples of needs. You don't have to wish for them; they help you every single day. Everyone needs certain things: meals, something to drink, a place to live, clean clothes, and shoes that fit so your feet are protected as you run and play. If you ever felt hungry, thirsty, or cold, you already know how important needs are.

A "want" is something you might like, but it isn't needed for living or staying well. Wants are fun! They could be action figures, magic slime, sticker books, the coolest sneakers you saw at the store, or the sparkly pencil case you saw in your friend's bag. You can live without these things, even if you might really wish for them. Wants often make us smile, but life goes on just fine without them.

Let's picture a real-life day. Mia heads to school with two dollars in her pocket. At the store after class, she sees a sandwich and a new pack of colorful pens. She thinks, "Should I get food or the pens?" Food is a need; she'll get hungry if she skips lunch. The pens are a want, they look neat, but she already has another pack in her bag. If Mia spends her money on the sandwich, she feels full, and her body gets the energy it needs. If she chooses the new pens and misses lunch, her stomach will rumble later, and she'll wish she picked differently. Having a choice is exciting, but seeing the difference makes it easier. What would you do in Mia's place?

Try this quick game—close your eyes and think of the last thing you asked someone to buy for you. Was it something you absolutely had to have, or was it just for fun? Here are several tips to help you distinguish between the options:

- Do I need this to be healthy or safe?
- Would my life be tricky or uncomfortable without it?
- Is it something I'll use every day?
- Could I wait until later to get it, or is it for right now?

If you answered yes to most of these questions, you likely have an unmet need. If not, it's likely a want.

Let's look at some examples you might know.

Things Kids Need

- Lunch for school
- Toothbrush and toothpaste
- Water bottle
- Warm coat in winter
- School shoes
- A bed to sleep in

Things Kids Want

- Extra large ice cream cone
- Fancy phone case
- Movie tickets for the weekend

- Super fast remote-control car
- Glittery hair bands
- Newest trendy backpack (when yours still works fine)

Wants can sound fun, and everyone loves them. There's no rule that says you can never have wants! In fact, saving up for something special is a great way to feel proud of your choices. But here's the smartest trick: take care of your needs first, and you will always have what your body and mind need to grow happy and strong.

If you ever feel stuck, try asking yourself, "If I buy this now, will I have enough left for what I really need?" Imagine if all your lunch money is used on sweets, but then you feel tired and hungry during your soccer game. That's why meeting your needs before your wants is a wise habit grown-ups use too.

Here's a little challenge: You have just enough for either a raincoat or a cool new video game. It's the rainy season, and your old coat has holes. Which will help you more each day? Can you save up later for the game?

Kids who ask these questions are already learning how to make choices like money superheroes. And once you know the difference between needs and wants, you're ready to start spending smart, not silly!

Smart Spending Strategies and a Cautionary Tale

Knowing the difference between wants and needs is like having a secret tool in your pocket whenever you have money to spend. When you understand what you really have to buy versus what would just be fun, it's much easier to decide what should come first. Imagine you have ten dollars. You're walking through a store, and your eyes catch a glittery set of stickers, then a squishy toy, and then a small bag of your favorite candy. It's easy to want everything all at once! But some things, like new markers for school, might be something you need, while those fun extras are wants. Taking a second to notice this can change the way you spend your money.

Here's what can happen if you don't stop and think. One Saturday, Max gets ten dollars for helping his neighbor wash her car. He's feeling like a star, with crisp bills in his pocket. At the store, Max's heart pounds when he passes a box of action figures. He grabs one in a snap! That's four dollars gone. At the checkout line, a spinning top catches his eye. He pauses for a second, remembers seeing videos of it online, and thinks, "I have to try it!" Plop, another three dollars spent. On the way out, he smells popcorn, and before he knows it, he's munching, handing the rest of his money to the cashier. Max feels amazing, almost like he's on top of the world—until his excitement fizzles out once he's home.

That afternoon, Max hears his friends talking about a weekend trip to the ice skating rink. Everyone's planning to go, and Max is keen to join them. His mom says, "It's five dollars; do you have enough?" Max's stomach drops. He checks his wallet - empty. All his money is gone, spent on things he didn't really need. "I wish I had saved some," he says quietly. The squishy toy is already lost under the couch. The action figure is fun, but his friends are heading out without him. It feels disappointing not having enough for something he really wants to do.

Max's story is a little like what happens to many people, or, kids and adults both! Sometimes, there's lots of excitement in spending fast. But when the money is gone, it can leave you wishing you'd made different choices. That's why practicing smart spending is an enormous help. It lets you do more of what you want, not just now, but later, too.

Smart spending starts even before you enter a store or open your wallet. Here are some steps to try each time you have money to spend:

Make a Super Simple Wish List

- Write down what you want and what you need.
- Put stars next to things that are needs.
- Look at your list and think: If I only have this much money, what should I get first?

Compare Before You Buy

- Check prices in the store or online.
- Ask yourself: Is this the best deal, or could I find it somewhere else for less?

Pause and Ask Yourself

- Do I really want this, or do I just see it right now and feel excited?
- Will I still want this next week, or is it something I only want today?

Talk With Someone You Trust

- Ask a parent, grandparent, or teacher what they would do.
- Sometimes talking it over helps you see things in a new way.
- Grown-ups can share stories about times they wished they had spent their money differently.

Set Aside a Bit for Later

- Try putting one or two dollars aside each time you get money.
- Soon, you'll have enough for a bigger wish that means more to you.

Here's a quick checklist for your next spending adventure:

- Did I list my wants and needs first?
- Did I check prices and compare?
- Did I wait a moment, or did I just grab-and-go?
- Did I talk to someone before making a choice?
- Did I leave a bit for later, just in case?

Making these steps a habit can turn smart spending into a personal superpower. Each time you use your money, you learn more about what matters most to you. Even better, it feels great when you still have enough for something special down the road. Playing money games and role-playing smart shopping with friends or family is a fun way to practice. Pretty soon you'll get a chance to try out your skills in a real-life game where your choices can pay off, so get ready for some smart, playful spending!

Interactive 'Needs vs. Wants' Game Activity

Remember what happened in the story when our friend spent all their money on things they wanted, instead of what they truly needed? It can be easy to pick something fun and exciting in the moment, but it's much harder when you realize you haven't saved enough for the things that actually matter. Earlier in this chapter, you learned why it's smart to save your money for things that really matter. This game helps you practice that idea, so next time you make a choice, you'll remember what's most important.

Let's explore how to make smart choices with a fun "Needs vs. Wants" game you can try on your own. First, you'll need some paper to write on, or you can use this page if your book allows it. Grab a pencil too. Now, before we get started, let's talk about what a "need" is and what a "want" is. A "need" is something you must have, or things that help you live and stay healthy, like food, water, a place to sleep, or shoes that fit for walking to school. A "want" is something you would like to have, but you could do just fine without it. For example, a sandwich when you're hungry is a need. But getting a second ice cream cone, just because it looks yummy, is a want.

Here's how to play the game: You will see a list of things on your page, or you can make up your list right now. Some things on the list are true needs (things that help you be safe, healthy, and ready for your day), and other things are wants (items that are extra, fun, or just for treats). Take a look at each item one at a time. Circle every item you truly need—that means you can't do well without it right now. Put a big X on the things that are helpful, fun, or just extra for you at this moment.

Here are some examples to practice with:

- Shoes that fit your feet
- Lunch for school
- Video game set
- Water bottle for sports
- A giant bag of candy
- Warm winter coat
- Movie tickets
- New pencils for homework

Let's reason through a few together. Imagine "new pencils for homework" is on your list. If you don't have a pencil, you can't finish your homework, so you should circle this item because it is necessary. Now, let's think about the "giant bag of candy." Is it really necessary, even if it's fun to share with friends or have at a party? Not really, so that's where you'll put an X. Shoes that fit your feet help you walk and go to school, so circle them. What about "movie tickets"? It's fun to see a movie, but if you don't see one today, you can wait so that one gets an X.

Try to go through your whole list now. As you look at each thing, ask yourself, "If I spent my money on this, would I have enough for what I need later?" Maybe pause for a moment and think about how you'd feel if you got everything you wanted, but then, when you needed lunch or a coat, you ran out of money. Would you feel a little worried, or maybe wish you could go back and change your mind? That's why it makes a big difference to think before you spend.

After you finish circling and crossing off, take another moment to look over your list. Were any of your choices challenging to make? Maybe you found yourself really wanting that new video game, but you also know you really need new sneakers for gym class. You can talk about your list with someone you trust, a friend, your parent, or your teacher. Did you both put an X on the same things, or were your ideas different? Sometimes even grown-ups don't always agree on what's a need and what's a want, so it's great to hear other people's thoughts.

Did anything on the list surprise you? Was there an item, like a lunchbox with your favorite cartoon characters, that seemed tricky? Both a plain lunchbox and a fancy one do the same job, so the plain one would be a need, and the cartoon one is a want; it's special, but not needed. If you have extra money, save it, but if you only have enough for one, pick the one that helps most.

Playing this game helps you see where your money might go each day. Maybe some choices are easier than others. Maybe you notice you circled a lot, and that could mean you have to go back and pick the most important needs first. That's part of the real-life choices you and everyone else make, and it helps you save for big things, like a school field trip or a birthday present for someone you care about. Every time you make choices like these, you're getting better at knowing what matters most and making your money work for you.

Now that you understand the difference between wants and needs, you're ready to become a money superhero by making smart choices with your coins. Remember, thinking before you spend helps you make sure your needs come first so you stay healthy and happy, and saving a little can help you get special things later too. By practicing these ideas through fun games and everyday decisions, you'll feel proud of how you use your money, not just today, but for many adventures ahead!

CHAPTER 5
BUDGETING - YOUR MONEY PLAN
YOUR MONEY PLAN

"Mom, can I buy the new game now?" Jamie asked, eyes wide and hopeful. The answer wasn't a simple yes or no. Instead, Jamie's mom smiled and pulled out a colorful sheet of paper covered in bright markers. "Let's see where your money is going first," she said. Jamie watched as they wrote down numbers and colors, turning scattered coins and bills into a plan. It was like giving each dollar its own job, a team working together toward something special.

That moment changed everything. Suddenly, money wasn't just pieces of paper and shiny coins disappearing fast. It was a puzzle to solve, a story unfolding with every choice made. For kids like Jamie, and maybe for you, this kind of planning turns wishes into real things you can hold, from sticker books to skateboard wheels. Sometimes it means saving up slowly, other times figuring out smart ways to stretch your dollars without missing out on fun.

Money isn't magic, but knowing what happens to it can feel pretty close. And just like Jamie learned, understanding how to handle your money is one of the coolest skills you can have. It all starts with a simple question: Where does your money go?

Understanding Budgets and Tracking Your Money

Picture this: What if your money was a team? Would you rather have every dollar you earn sprint off in a different direction; one going to candy, one to a lost sock, another hiding somewhere in your backpack, or, would you want your money working together like a team, aiming for a win? That's what a budget does. It's like a treasure map for your money. It helps you see where your coins and bills go, so you're not left wondering why your pockets are empty when you really want that new game or book.

Imagine you earn money in little bits here and there. You might get an allowance for emptying the dishwasher. You could find a shiny $5 bill tucked into a birthday card. Maybe you rake leaves for the neighbor or help your aunt carry groceries. All these small amounts add up: that's your income, or the total money you bring in. Seeing all the ways money comes in is the very first step in building your budget map.

Let's meet Jamie. Jamie gets $5 each week for helping with chores. Some weeks, Jamie walks dogs for $3 extra. Then comes birthday time: a $10 bill slides out of a card. Jamie puts all this money together to see what the total is. The next move is to figure out where the money goes. Jamie likes snacks at the corner store, wants to buy a cool sticker book, and saves up for a remote-control car that costs $30.

Jamie's basic budget might start like this:

- $5 allowance (weekly)
- $3 dog-walking (sometimes)
- $10 birthday gift (one time)

Jamie writes down everything on a bright sheet of paper, using markers for each section. Imagine the income in green, spending in red, and saving in blue. It starts feeling like a game, where every dollar is a player on the team. Each player needs to know its job.

Jamie knows that $4 each week often goes to snacks and sweets. After buying snacks, Jamie has $6 left one week because of the birthday money. Jamie wants to make sure some money goes into a piggy bank. Putting $3 aside for saving means Jamie doesn't spend everything at once. That last $3 can be set aside for something bigger, like saving for that remote-control car. Week after week, Jamie adds to the car fund, and soon those dollars begin to add up.

Why track all this?

Think about trying to build a tower made of blocks, but your blocks are scattered all over the house. It's hard to build anything strong if you don't know where your building pieces are. When you track your money, you start seeing patterns. You can spot if you spend most of your money on snacks, saving nothing, or if you put too much away and forget to have any fun. By making a chart or drawing a simple budget map, you get to see your money story at a glance.

Interactive Money Map

Try making your own money plan at home. Grab a big piece of paper and some colored pencils or markers. Draw three boxes and label them “Money In,” “Money Out,” and “Saving Up.” Every time money comes in, write it in the first box. For every snack, toy, or game you buy, jot it down in the “Money Out” box. Any coins or bills that you save for something special should be placed in the "Saving Up" container. For extra fun, turn it into a board game. Move a playing piece toward a prize every time you save a dollar. The closer your piece gets to the finish line, the closer you are to reaching your goal.

Spending Isn’t the Enemy

Some people think budgets are just about saying “no” all the time. Actually, a budget helps you say “yes” to things you care about. You get to plan for treats, books, crafts, or saving for something amazing. Controlling your money doesn’t mean you skip out on the fun. It means you have the freedom to allocate your money wisely, preventing unexpected expenses or wishing for things you could have planned for.

What if you want a new skateboard that costs $40? A budget helps you see how much you have, how long it will take to save the rest, and what small changes you can make to speed it up. Maybe you skip a small snack once in a while and slide those coins into your goal fund.

Budgets help you feel in charge, like a team captain calling the plays. Every dollar gets told where to go. Pretty soon, you’ll see your money working together, helping you score the things you want most. Some kids have used their budgets to buy something they really wanted, like the day Jamie finally bought that remote-control car with money saved up one week at a time. Budgeting makes reaching goals possible, and your next win could be just around the corner.

A Real-Life Kid's Budgeting Success Story

It started on the first Saturday of spring. Leo was riding his skateboard past Buzzy's Bike Shop when he spotted something amazing in the window a bright blue bicycle with thick tires and sparkly silver handlebars. He pressed his nose to the glass and stared, picturing all the places he'd go if that bike was really his. There was a tag. $80.

Leo knew his old bike was getting too small for him. The blue bike looked like it could take him over bumps, zoom down hills, and even keep up with his older sister on their trips to the park. He ran home, his mind busy with ideas. At the kitchen table, Leo pulled out a pad and scribbled, "I want the blue bike from Buzzy's. Cost: $80." He felt excited but a little worried, too. That was a lot of money.

His mom poured a glass of milk and sat beside him. "Big goal, huh?" she smiled. "How about we make a money plan together?" Leo nodded. He liked the word plan. It sounded possible.

The next thing Leo did was figure out how much money he already had. He shook his piggy bank, and out tumbled coins and a few crumpled bills - $12.75. Not a bad start, but still a long way to go. Leo's allowance was $5 each week if he took out the garbage, fed the dog, and stayed on top of his homework. Sometimes he earned extra money by weeding the neighbor's garden or helping Grandpa wash the car. He wrote everything down on his paper.

Leo grabbed his pencil again and made a list:

- Bike cost: $80
- Money already saved: $12.75
- Allowance each week: $5
- Possible extra jobs: $3 for car wash, $2 for weeding

He tapped his pencil. If he saved all his allowance, he'd still need more than thirteen weeks. That seemed like forever. Mom nudged him, "What could help you save faster?" Leo thought about snacks from the corner store and remembered the toy cars he sometimes bought just because he liked how they looked, even though he hardly played with them. He drew another list:

Ways to Save More Each Week

- Skip buying snacks after school: save $2
- Don't buy toy cars for a while: save $3
- Do extra chores for neighbors: maybe earn $2
- Save birthday money from Grandma: could be $10

If he added up the savings from skipping snacks and toys, Leo figured he could save an extra $5 each week. That made everything look brighter. He started to feel like reaching his goal wasn't just a dream.

The next day, Leo made a colorful chart for his wall. He drew 80 boxes, one for each dollar he needed. Every time he saved or earned a dollar, he colored in another box with a red marker. Sometimes, he even drew tiny bicycle wheels in the boxes. Dark clouds rolled in a few times. One Friday, while out with friends, banana ice cream smelled so good he almost used his money. He squeezed his fist in his pocket and thought about the blue bike. Instead, he came home, put that $2 right in his savings jar, and colored in two more boxes.

When chores felt boring or his friends went to the movies, Leo would take out his paper and see his plan. Looking at the jar filled with coins and the chart filling with color made him smile. He even drew a picture of the blue bike and taped it to the front of his jar as a reminder to stick with it.

After seven weeks, plus a birthday, several car washes with Grandpa, and a lot of skipped snack days, the numbers on Leo's paper matched the price in Buzzy's window. He could hardly believe it as he held the worn bills and a baggie of quarters. Buying the bike felt like an adventure coming true. As the shop owner put the shiny bike into his hands, Leo felt a warm, proud feeling bubble inside.

He realized every little choice added up, and sticking to his plan made the celebration extra sweet. On the way home, wind in his face, he caught himself grinning. Maybe you're wishing for something special, too. It all starts with a simple plan, a little patience, and some small steps. Just picture your dream and imagine the exciting path your money plan could show you.

Interactive Activity: My Budget Worksheet

Seeing another kid reach their money goal by making a plan proves that having a budget really works. Anyone can use these same simple steps to save up for what they want, whether it's a new game, a trip, or even a small treat. Making a budget is just like giving your money special jobs. You can save for something great, buy something now, or help a friend or someone in need. Each person's budget will be their adventure, because we all care about different things and have different dreams.

The "My Budget" worksheet is a tool for turning these dreams into real-life goals. It's not a test or homework; it's the start of your money adventure. The worksheet is like a treasure map, showing you your path to reaching what matters most to you.

Begin by placing your financial goal at the top of the page. A money goal is your personal mission. For example, maybe you want a new soccer ball. That's your mission: save up enough for the ball. Just like the kid who saved for a bike one week at a time, your goal is something you want enough that you're willing to make a plan. Whatever you pick, write it big so you can always see what you're aiming for.

Next comes figuring out how much money you have to work with. Think about where your money comes from. Maybe it's a weekly allowance, gifts for your birthday, money for doing special chores, or even spare change you find around the house. Add up these amounts. For instance, let's say you get $2 a week for allowance and $10 on your birthday. That means this month, you might have $18 total. Write your total number proudly on your worksheet; this is the treasure you start with.

The big question is: how will you use it? The worksheet is split into three boxes: Save, Spend, and Share. For each box, there's a way to make fun choices about what you want to do.

Saving means putting aside a little bit now for a bigger reward later. If your soccer ball costs $15, and you save $5 each week, you can reach your goal in just three weeks. Maybe you decide to save $1 each week instead, and it takes a little longer; that's okay, too. The main thing is to write down how much you plan to save and what you're saving for.

Spending is about picking treats or small things you enjoy right now. In the spending box, you can list what you like: maybe a snack after school, a sticker at the shop, or a small toy. If you spend $1 each week, write it down, and think of what makes you happy to use that money on.

Sharing is one of the most powerful boxes on your worksheet. Sharing can mean donating a dollar at a charity drive, helping buy art supplies for the class, or even picking out a small gift for someone else. Write down how much you want to share and where you want it to go. Even giving a little can make a big difference.

Once you've filled in the numbers, it's time to make your budget pop. Open your colored pencils, markers, or crayons and get creative. Color in each box with a different bright color. Draw your money goal: a soccer ball for saving, a slice of pizza for spending, and a heart for sharing. You could even make a rainbow in the background or draw yourself reaching your goal. Decorating your worksheet makes the plan feel more special, and it will help you remember your choices every time you see it.

Put your finished worksheet somewhere you'll see it, like a wall, the fridge, inside your backpack, or your special drawer. This helps remind you what you're working towards and keeps you excited. If things change, maybe you get more money from a surprise gift or you want your goal to be something new, you can always start a fresh worksheet. Budgets aren't about being perfect; they're about practicing making choices.

Even grownups use budgets to help plan for vacations, groceries, or birthday parties. Learning now is like building your own superpower. Every time you use your worksheet, you get better at making choices, and you'll find it becomes easier. The first step is just starting with a simple, colorful budget. Each time you reach a money goal or follow your plan, you're taking charge of your own adventures and showing that smart money skills are for everyone.

Now that you know how to build a budget, track your money, and make smart choices about saving and spending, you're ready to take control of your own money adventure. Remember, every dollar is like a teammate helping you reach your goals, whether it's a new game, a bike, or something special just for you. By planning where your money goes and keeping an eye on it with your colorful charts and worksheets, you can turn small steps into big wins. So grab your markers, start your money map, and watch how practicing these simple habits can help you save, spend, and share in ways that feel fun and exciting. Your money story is just beginning. What will you choose to do next?

CHAPTER 6
GIVING BACK—SHARING IS CARING

What if I told you that money isn't just for buying toys, games, or treats? Most people consider money to be something only to spend on themselves, but it can actually do a lot more. Money can be used to help others, make a difference in your community, and bring smiles to people and animals who need a little extra care.

In this chapter, we'll explore how even small amounts of money can turn into acts of kindness that spread far beyond what you might expect. You'll hear stories of kids using their ideas and coins to make the world a better place and discover simple ways you can start giving back, too. Whether it's through sharing money, time, or thoughtful actions, you'll see how giving shows that caring really counts no matter your age or how much you have.

The Power of Giving: Why Sharing Matters

Imagine you had a handful of dollars and a pocket full of ideas. Most of the time, you might dream about buying a new game, a toy, or some cool markers for your art projects. There's something extra special about discovering that your money could do more than bring you fun stuff. It could actually help someone else, or even a bunch of someones. Money is more than coins and bills; it can also be a way to send care to people, animals, or places that need it.

Picture this: a friend's puppy gets a new warm blanket at the shelter, a lonely cat now purrs with a shiny toy, or the garden around your school bursts with new flowers because you bought seeds. That's money transforming into pure kindness. And the coolest part? You don't have to be a grown-up to make this magic happen.

Meet Max, age 9. One rainy Saturday, Max and his mom stopped by the local animal shelter to drop off some old newspapers for the cats. Max wandered down the hallway, peeking into the rooms where dogs wagged their tails and cats blinked sleepy eyes at him. He noticed that some animal beds looked flat and shaggy, and a sign near the door said, "Blankets needed. Will you help us keep our pets warm and cozy?"

Max couldn't stop thinking about those animals and their scruffy beds on the ride home. Later, he asked his mom how he might help the shelter get more blankets. His mom said that donations always help, but Max's piggy bank only held eight dollars. That's when he came up with a plan.

He decided to start a "Blankets for Buddies" project. First, Max counted every penny from his allowance and loose change, then asked family members if they wanted to chip in. His older sister added two dollars, his grandma gave him some soft fleece fabric, and his dad showed him how to make a simple flyer using bright markers. Max hung up his flyers at school and on his street, telling people he was collecting money and cozy blankets for shelter pets.

A week later, Max and his mom set up a lemonade stand on their block. He made a big sign that read, "Buy a Cup, Help a Pup!" and promised that every dollar would go to the animal shelter. Some neighbors came just for lemonade, but others gave extra money because they liked Max's caring idea. At the end of the day, he counted over twenty-five dollars in the jar. On Sunday, Max used his earnings to buy five fluffy blankets at a discount store and brought along the ones his grandma made.

When the shelter staff saw Max's arms loaded with soft new blankets and a big bag of coins, their faces lit up. A volunteer showed Max how each dog now had a clean, warm place to rest. One shy puppy even curled up right away and started snoring. Max snapped a picture for his school and felt a bubbly warmth inside his chest.

It didn't stop with blankets and lemonade. Max's friends saw his project posted in the school hallway and wanted to join in. The next month, two of them collected food and made homemade cat toys. Another friend started bringing in old towels. Watching Max and others work together made more people at school, parents, and even teachers notice ways they could help, too.

Kindness works almost like skipping stones across a pond. Every time Max or his friends did something to help, it spread out, and more people felt happy and wanted to do their part. Even small gifts turned into bigger changes for every animal and person involved. Plus, Max felt taller and bolder, like someone who made real waves in the world. He learned he could be a helper, and helping made him feel proud.

When you do something nice, even with a little bit of money or a simple idea, you don't just help one puppy or one place. You set off a ripple. Your kindness might inspire your friends, your family, or even people you don't know yet. Maybe you only have a few coins, or maybe you're better at making homemade treats or drawing cards to cheer someone up. The size of your gift doesn't matter; the caring you share is what really counts. What are some small ways you might care for others, even if you don't have much to give? Could your next birthday party be a time to collect donations, or could you organize a fun group project with your class? The world is waiting to see what you'll try next.

Small Acts, Big Impact: How Even Little Giving Counts

When a kid gives money to help shelter animals, it means more than just dropping coins in a jar. It shows that anyone can be a helper. Imagine you have only a few coins left in your pocket. Some kids think, "What difference could this tiny amount make?" But here's a secret: every single coin, smile, or thoughtful act has the power to brighten someone's day.

You don't have to wait until you're grown up or have a big pile of money to start changing the world. Sometimes, kindness is as simple as cleaning out your toy box and finding toys you do not play with anymore. If you place those toys in a donation box, you're offering someone else a reason to grin. Picture a child picking out your old race car or stuffed animal as their new favorite. That small act feels warm inside, like a hug passing from you to them.

How Kids Can Share Every Day

Easy Ways to Give

- Drop loose coins into the donation jar at the grocery store.
- Collect school supplies or books you no longer need and give them to your school's sharing shelf.
- Help your class organize a mini bake sale, selling cookies or muffins, and send what you earn to help people or animals.

These ideas do not need a lot of time or planning. You can do them with friends, with your family, or even by yourself. Standing in front of the donation box, you can feel proud, knowing that even a single coin or a dollar can help buy food for a shelter, or books for a classroom.

Helping with Your Time

Money is not the only thing that matters when you want to help others. You have something even bigger - your time, your smiles, and your ideas!

- Offer to read your favorite storybook to your younger brother or sister. When you read each page, they might giggle or ask you questions. You help them feel special and learn something new.
- Team up with your neighbors to pick up litter in the park. Each piece of trash you pick up keeps your world cleaner. People who walk by will notice what you're doing and feel grateful.
- Write a cheerful note to someone who might be having a difficult day. You could decorate a card with stickers or a funny drawing, then give it to your teacher, bus driver, or even someone in your family. Imagine the smile when they read your words!

Every time you offer your time, you make a mark that lasts. Even grown-ups remember when someone took a moment to be kind to them.

Feeling What Others Might Feel

It's fun to imagine what the people you help might think. Someone finding your donated book could feel excited to read a new story. A nurse who receives your thank-you card might put it on the wall beside her desk so she never forgets that she's helped someone like you. Friends playing in the park could giggle because their shoes don't get dirty from trash, all thanks to your cleanup effort.

On the other hand, you might notice something too. Helping others can make your own heart feel lighter. Maybe you start your day with a yawn, but after sharing or giving back, you feel more awake, more cheerful, and even a bit taller inside.

More Ideas You Can Try

- Make decorations for your school or classroom to bring a splash of color, especially on tough days.
- Invite kids who are alone at school to join your game or activity.
- Save a tiny bit from your weekly allowance in a jar marked "Helping Fund" and use it when you spot a cause you care about.
- Donate outgrown coats, hats, or gloves during a winter drive.
- Share a homemade treat with someone new, or give your neighbor's pet a gentle pat.

Kids can also come up with causes that matter most to them. Maybe you love animals and want to help the animal shelter, or you feel sad when someone in your class seems lonely. Think of ways you can make a difference for them. You might be surprised at how many things you notice once you start investigating how to help.

Remember, giving is not just about stuff or money. It's about sharing ideas, showing you care, and using your time to make someone's world a little better. Your kindness is as big as anyone's, no matter how old you are or how much you have.

Now comes the fun part: start imagining what you care most about helping. Is there a problem at school, at home, or in your neighborhood that makes you think, "I wish I could help"? Soon, you'll get the chance to create your own plan to make a difference. Which cause will you choose? Your story as a helper is only just beginning.

Make Your Mark: Creating a Personal Giving Plan

Now that you know how your acts of kindness, no matter how small, can be powerful, let's make your own plan to help others really come alive! Imagine having a plan that's all about sharing your best ideas to brighten up your world, one simple step at a time. This is called a "Giving Plan." Making a Giving Plan means you're choosing to make kindness something you do on purpose, not just every once in a while when you remember. It turns positive thoughts into actual things you can pick up, check off, and say, "Hey, I did that!"

A Giving Plan is just your special guide for helping others. It doesn't have to be huge or fancy. It's made by you and for you. You can choose what matters most to you and how to act on it. Some people love helping animals. Others might want to clean up their neighborhood park, write cheerful notes to people who need a smile, or collect clothes for families who don't have enough. Now it's your turn to think about what makes you want to make things better.

Start by sitting comfortably and letting your mind wander. Who or what would you most love to help? Is there a cause that feels important to you or a place you want to make brighter? Some ideas could be walking dogs at a shelter, helping your community by collecting extra food for people who need it, making cards for lonely neighbors, or planting trees to help the planet. Write all your ideas down on a piece of paper or in your notebook. You can doodle, use stickers, or write just a few words. Take about two or three minutes and don't worry if you have a big list or just a few items. Every idea is welcome!

Look over your brainstorming sheet and choose the one thing that pops out at you, makes you smile, or feels exciting. Maybe you keep thinking about making care packages for children at a hospital, or you want to help clean your school playground. Circle the cause or write it in bold letters at the center of a poster or piece of paper. This is going to be the heart of your Giving Plan.

Get creative! Decorate your paper or poster so it shows what your cause is about. Draw pictures, add colorful borders, or glue on magazine cutouts. If your plan is about helping animals, you could draw a big joyful dog or a fish swimming through blue waves. If you chose to help your community by collecting coats, consider including images of smiling kids putting on warm jackets. Use your favorite markers, crayons, or paints. The more it looks like you, the better!

Think about what a good goal for your plan could be. Your goal can be small, like "I will pick up five pieces of trash in the park this week" or "I will make one poster to teach others about recycling." It could also be a little bigger, like "I will collect five cans of food for the local food shelf." The most important thing is to choose a realistic goal you can achieve. Even one helpful action is important and can change someone's day for the better!

Now write down two or three concrete actions you'll take. For example, if your plan is to help animals, you could: 1) ask your family to go with you to visit the animal shelter, 2) make homemade dog treats to donate, 3) tell your class about why animal care matters. If you can't give money or things, think of ways to give your time. You might draw cheerful pictures for older people, start a kindness club with your friends, or ask your family if you can help rake leaves for a neighbor.

Remember, you don't have to do this on your own. Ask family, friends, or your teacher for ideas on how to start or improve your plan. Invite a friend to join you; sometimes helping together feels even better!

Once your plan is ready, hang your poster or giving plan in a place you'll see it often, like on your bedroom wall or refrigerator. Every time you look at it, let yourself feel proud and remember why you wanted to help. Pause for a moment and picture the smiles your actions can bring. Imagine a neighbor feeling less lonely because you shared a drawing or a child feeling cared for because they have a warm coat.

Every Giving Plan is special because it's about what matters to you. Think of the boy who gathered canned food and saw his mountain of donations grow just because he asked his class to help. Remember the girl who spent an hour each week picking up trash in the park; she made her neighborhood cleaner and felt great doing it. Now, as you carry out your Giving Plan, you'll not only help others but learn something about yourself too. Maybe you'll discover that helping makes you feel happy, proud, and connected, or maybe your idea will inspire others to do something kind. Small plans can spark big changes, and your journey starts today.

Now that you've seen how even a little money or a small act of kindness can grow into something amazing, it's your turn to take the first step. Whether you give a few coins, share your time, or start a fun project like Max, you have the power to make a real difference for people, animals, and places you care about. Remember, giving isn't just about what you have; it's about caring and sharing from the heart. So go ahead, dream up your own plan, gather your ideas, and watch how your kindness can spread, because when you help others, you're also helping yourself grow into someone brave, thoughtful, and proud. Your journey as a helper is just beginning, and the world is waiting to see all the good you'll do!

CHAPTER 7

GROWING YOUR MONEY LIKE MAGIC

Have you ever wondered how money can grow all by itself without you doing any extra work? What if your savings could turn into more money just by sitting quietly in a bank? Or have you thought about how some people make their money multiply faster through clever choices? These might sound like secrets or magic tricks, but they are actually simple ideas that anyone can understand, even kids like you!

In this chapter, we will explore how your money can start growing on its own using something called interest and the basics of investing. You'll discover how saving a little bit can lead to bigger rewards over time, and you'll get to try a fun activity that shows how money grows week by week. By the end, you'll see that growing your money isn't just for grown-ups, it's a kind of magic you can learn and watch happen for yourself!

The Secret of Sleeping Money: Understanding Interest

Money may look quiet sitting in your piggy bank or wallet, but it has a special secret. Money can actually grow, almost like magic, if you know where to put it. Imagine you have ten shiny coins. You put them in a box, and when you open the box later - surprise! There's an extra coin inside. It's not a trick. It's something called "interest."

Kids often think money just stays the same. You spend it or you save it, and that's it. But there's another way to look at it. Think of your money as seeds that you can plant. When you put these seeds in the right place, they don't just stay seeds, they turn into a little plant that gets bigger every time you peek at it. A bank account is one of those special places. It's like a safe garden bed for your savings.

Banks love getting your money seeds, and they want to thank you for planting them with them. When you open a savings account and deposit your allowance, birthday cash, or spare change, the bank gives you a reward for letting your money rest there. This reward is called "interest." Interest is like getting a bonus just because your money is hanging out in the bank, waiting for you.

How does the bank have money to give you more? Banks use your money seeds for a while, almost the way a friend might borrow your ball for a game and then gives it back with a sticker as a thank you. When lots of people put money in the bank, the bank lends some of it to other people who need it, maybe someone starting a lemonade stand or buying a bicycle.

For letting the bank use your savings, they give you a little gift in return. That gift is interest.

Let's look at how it works with numbers you can picture. Say you get $10 for your birthday. You decide to leave it in your savings account instead of buying all the gummy worms at the store. At the end of the month, the bank gives you an extra $0.10 as interest. You didn't work for this dime. You didn't have to do chores or sell cookies. The bank adds the interest for you while you wait. Now your $10 has turned into $10.10!

Here's a story about Sam. Sam really wanted a new soccer ball. She could just spend her $10 right away, but she was curious to see what would happen if she let it sit in the bank. Every month, a little more money showed up. It felt like her coins were working together and making baby coins. She watched her savings grow in her bankbook and made a chart with stickers for every time the number went up. Each time, she felt proud not just for saving but for seeing her money do something special.

You can make your own interest tracker. Take a piece of paper, draw ten squares for your ten dollars, and add another tiny square every time your bank sends you interest. Over the months, your row of squares grows longer. In games and stories, we love to watch treasures get bigger, like a treasure chest slowly filling up with gold, isn't it exciting when your money does that too?

Interest may start small, but over time those extra coins and dollars build up. Every month your new total gets a little boost. The more patient you are, the more you will see your money grow. This teaches patience, planning, and pride. When kids watch their savings increase, they get confident. Saving isn't just about not spending, sometimes, it's also about letting your money become helpful and active all on its own.

And there are even more magical ways that money can grow. Just like some seeds turn into giant sunflowers, some ways of saving can make your money get bigger faster. Imagine hearing about secret treasure maps or stories of magic money trees. These are not just fairy tales with something called "investing," your money can grow strong branches and roots, too. By learning the basics and giving your savings time to grow, you're getting ready for new adventures in money magic. There's a whole world of secrets, stories, and simple tricks to explore, and you're about to become the hero of your own money story.

The Magic Money Tree: Investing Basics and How Savings Grow

Have you ever thought about what happens to your money after you put it in a safe place? Imagine this: money can actually grow all by itself even while you're asleep! It's like discovering a secret treasure in your own piggy bank. Now, your adventure goes even further. There's a way you can help your money multiply faster, just by making some clever choices.

Picture yourself in a magical garden. In the middle stands a tiny seed that you just planted. You water it and wait. Days go by, and that seed grows little by little. Soon, you see a sprout, then leaves, and after a while, it's a full-grown tree. But here's the fun twist: this tree grows coins and dollar bills on its branches! This is your magic money tree, and you're the gardener.

Let's meet Mia. One day, she asks her grandfather, "What happens if I plant a magic coin in the backyard?" Her grandfather laughs softly and says, "Well, your backyard might not grow real coins, but let me tell you a secret. There is a way to plant your money so it grows. It's called investing." Mia's eyes grow wide. "Investing?" she wonders. "Is it like magic?" Her grandfather nods. "It can feel like magic, but really, it's all about making smart choices."

Now, what is an investment? Imagine you put your money in a place where it can turn into more money over time. It's not spooky or tricky. It just means putting your money somewhere special that can help it grow. Here's how it works for kids:

- If you open a **savings account** at a bank and put your birthday money in, you're planting your magic seed. The bank says thank you by adding a bit extra (called interest) to your money because you let them borrow it for a while.
- Sometimes, your family might talk about **stocks** or **bonds**. Imagine you own a tiny piece of a huge candy store. If the store does well and sells lots of candy, you might get a small piece of the profits. That's like your magic tree growing bigger branches. You don't have to be a grown-up to learn about stocks, there are even junior accounts made for kids.
- With a **certificate of deposit** or a junior account, you're promising to leave your money tucked away for a set time. Because you're such a patient saver, the bank rewards you with even more interest. These special accounts are like fertilizer for your money tree, making it sturdy and healthy.

Let's look at another example. Leo wonders, "What if I get $1 for my allowance and save it instead of buying candy?" He tries it out, putting his dollar in a savings account. After some time, his $1 turns into $1.10, then $1.20. If Leo adds another dollar every week, soon he has a pile that's even bigger. The more he adds, the more branches and leaves appear on his magic money tree.

Try imagining your tree. How tall is it? What kind of money fruit grows on its branches? Do you want shiny silver coins or crisp green bills? Every time you save, you're dropping another seed in the ground. Each seed will stretch up toward the sun and turn into a strong tree with lots of branches—and each branch brings even more money fruit.

Starting early can be the best magic trick. Think about planting apple seeds. The sooner you start, the bigger your apple tree grows. If you plant your money seeds now, you give them plenty of time to stretch and reach. For example, if you put away just $1, it could slowly become $2, then $4, then more. It doesn't happen in one day. It takes a little patience and lots of watering (saving a bit every week).

Let's play a game. What if you set a goal to save half your allowance each week? Every coin you add to your savings becomes like a drop of water for your magic money tree. After a few weeks or months, you look back and see how tall and leafy it's become. If you keep saving just a small amount, you'll notice your tree crowding with more and more money fruit.

Think about something you really want, maybe a bike, a favorite game, or a day at the amusement park. Can you picture your magic money tree helping you reach that dream? Would you plant different seeds or water your tree more often if it meant having enough for that wish? Your choices and habits serve as the sunshine and rain that nourish and strengthen your financial tree.

Imagine the experience of witnessing the growth of your magical money tree, week by week. What if you kept track of each new branch or coin? Your next adventure is waiting: a chance to see your magic money tree come to life and discover how much it can grow, just by being you.

Money Planting Challenge: Watch $10 Grow Every Week!

Imagine holding a tiny seed that could one day turn into a tree loaded with shiny coins. That's what happens with money when you start saving and add a little bit of magic called "interest." Right now, you've got a magic money tree seed in your pocket, and it's worth $10. Here's how we'll use that $10 to play a game and watch it grow, just like a little green sprout, with some pretend interest to make things extra fun. You'll grab some paper, pencils, and maybe your favorite colored markers. You'll become a money gardener, tracking every leaf that pops up as our money tree gets taller each week.

The first step is to get ready for the money-growing game. On your paper, make a table with three columns. The first one is called "Week," the second is "Starting Money," and the third is "Money After Interest." Draw Week 1 at the top, then Week 2, then Week 3, and keep going for at least eight weeks. If you like, doodle a tiny seed or sprout beside Week 1 and leave space next to each week to add bigger leaves or flowers as the money grows. You might want to pick green and gold colors to bring your chart to life.

Start the game by writing $10 in the "Starting Money" column for Week 1. This is your magic seed. Now choose how much your tree will grow each week. Let's use a 10% interest rate because it's easy for new gardeners. That means each week, your money gets 10% bigger. To figure out 10% of $10, think of it as moving the decimal over one place ($1.00). Now, add that to your first $10. Your "Money After Interest" for Week 1 becomes $11. That's your seed sprouting a tiny leaf.

Move to Week 2. Your new "Starting Money" is $11. What's 10% of $11? Grab your calculator or do the math step-by-step: $11 times 0.10 is $1.10. Add that to $11 and you get $12.10. Notice how the interest you add gets a little bigger each time, just like a tree grows more leaves as it gets taller.

Week 3 starts with $12.10. Find 10% of that ($1.21) and stack it on top ($12.10 plus $1.21 equals $13.31). Soon the numbers start growing faster. On your chart, draw a thicker stem or a branch bursting with little money leaves. Your money is still small, but you can spot your tree spreading out. Each time you fill in the chart for a new week, add a bit more color to the leaves, or maybe draw a bird or a bug for fun.

The coolest part is watching the totals go up, week after week. At first, the difference looks tiny. By Week 4, you'll have $14.64. In Week 5, $16.10. Each new bit of interest you add makes the next week's interest even bigger, and so on. This is called "compounding," and it works like rolling a tiny snowball down a hill until it grows super big.

Ask yourself: what could you buy if your tree keeps growing? After a while, you might have enough for a new game, a bike ride with friends, or maybe a big bag of candy to share. The game turns into a real quest when you try different tricks.

What if you start with $20 instead? Or try a 5% or 15% interest rate? Change the game, fill in your chart, and watch what twists happen to your money tree. You might end up with a skinny vine or a fat trunk bursting with coins.

If you want to play with real money one day, talk with a grown-up like your parents, a teacher, or even someone at a bank. Many adults use this very game by putting money in savings and letting interest grow it like magic. Their trees are called savings accounts or investments, and every dollar they put in acts just like your pretend seed.

Pay close attention as you write each new amount. See if your "garden" feels fuller. Sometimes growth moves slowly, but give it time and your tree will surprise you. Just like watering a plant every week and checking for new shoots, you get to see your money bloom right on your chart. Try adding doodles or stickers to make tracking fun. There's no perfect way; just have fun and watch your money seeds turn into flowers before your eyes.

Keep daydreaming about all the ways your money tree could grow. What if there were money vines for birthday gifts or bonus interest if you save every week without skipping? Make new charts and test your wildest ideas. The more you try, the more you'll see how saving and investing can bring little surprises, just like growing your very own magic tree, dollar by dollar.

Now that you know how money can grow all on its own through interest and smart saving, you're ready to become a true money gardener! By planting your savings carefully and watching your magic money tree grow taller with each new coin, you'll learn how patience and good choices help your treasure get bigger over time. Keep playing the money-growing game, trying new ideas, and asking questions. Soon, you'll discover even more exciting ways to make your money work for you. This is just the beginning of your adventure in money magic, and with what you've learned here, you're well on your way to becoming a confident saver and investor who can turn simple seeds into a whole forest of financial fun!

CHAPTER 8
WHAT ADULTS DO WITH MONEY

One afternoon, Anna watched as her mom sat at the kitchen table with a pile of colorful envelopes and a notebook. She was counting coins, marking off items on a list, and talking quietly with her dad about what to buy for the week. Anna's little brother asked if they could get ice cream, but Mom just smiled and said, "We'll see." Anna wondered why some things had to wait, even when they seemed like fun or treats. She didn't realize that every penny in those envelopes had a job to do, helping keep their home warm, food in the fridge, and plans for special days ahead. Money might look simple, just coins and bills, but behind it were many choices and careful thinking that adults do all the time, sometimes even without you noticing.

How Adults Use Money Every Day

There's a lot of work grown-ups do with money every single day, and you probably see some of it without really thinking about what's happening. In the morning, there might be bills on the table or someone finding a shopping list and checking what's in the fridge. Adults use money to keep a family comfortable and safe, and almost everything at home connects to this. For example, when the lights turn on, it's because an adult paid the electricity bill. When the refrigerator is full of apples, milk, and cheese, that means someone went to the store and made those choices while contemplating what the family needs most.

Inside every wallet or purse, there's a story about priorities. Say your parent just got paid after a week of working at their job. They might say, "This money has to last until next Friday." The first task is taking care of needs. That paycheck might get split up, with some going to pay rent so everyone has a place to sleep, some set aside for groceries like bread, carrots, and juice, and a piece saved for getting to work, like paying for bus passes or gas for the car.

Grown-ups don't just spend all the money right away. They often make a plan since things come first. That's why, when you ask about getting a big box of gummy bears or a new video game, sometimes the answer is, "Maybe later." It's not because adults don't want to say yes—it's because they're thinking about what has to come first. Buying food, paying for heating in the winter, making sure there are clean clothes, and paying for school supplies all matter a lot. If there's money left, then it's time to think about fun things, nicer snacks, or even something everyone can enjoy, like pizza night.

Every family has dreams and things to look forward to. Adults think about saving up bit by bit, just like you might put coins in a piggy bank for something special. Maybe there's a plan to buy new bikes, celebrate your birthday with your friends, or take a trip to your favorite park. Adults sometimes tuck away a small part of their money each week, even if it's just a little, because they know that small amounts grow over time. They try to plan for things you care about, so you can see that your own hopes matter, too.

But grown-ups don't always get to pick everything they want at once. Think about walking into the grocery store. There are so many choices, but Mom or Dad has a budget—that means there's a limit to how much they can spend. Maybe there's a choice between buying your favorite cereal or getting fruit for everyone's lunch. Sometimes the decision is between going out for burgers and fries, or putting that money toward saving for a movie night next week. It can feel tough to decide, but these choices help a family get what they need and sometimes even save for bigger treats later.

Let's peek a little deeper into a paycheck story. Imagine your parent comes home and sits down with you at the table. They explain, "I earned this from my job. First, we pay for where we live, so we always have a safe place. Next, we buy food and things we use every day like toothpaste and soap. Then, we pay bills for water and heat, and save a small amount for things that might surprise us. After that, whatever we have left helps us do something special or just have a bit of fun together." This way, you can see that every dollar has a job, and no dollar gets wasted.

Sometimes life surprises families. The washing machine breaks, someone gets the sniffles and needs a doctor, or the car needs gas earlier than planned. This is where grown-ups hope they have some money saved for emergencies. Saving up for just-in-case moments means saying "no" to more toys sometimes. When you hear "not right now," it's usually because your family is trying to make sure everyone is okay, even if something unexpected happens.

Seeing all these pieces can feel like looking at a puzzle. Every choice matters and helps keep the family safe and happy, with food on the table and lights shining. Next, you'll find out how families work together—sometimes kids can help, too—and how teamwork helps make plans, save for what matters, and is even part of the fun.

A Family's Money Story

Out in the living room, the Ramirez family settled onto the couch for their regular family meeting. Mom sat with her notebook open. Dad held a small stack of coins and some colorful envelopes. Mia and her little brother Lucas bounced on the cushions, curious about what they would talk about that night.

Mom started by smiling at everyone. "Okay, team, let's talk about our goal. We all wanted to save up for a family trip to Dino Land. Remember, we agreed to save a little bit each week." Lucas cheered, "I can't wait to see the giant dinosaur!" Mia raised her hand and asked, "But do we have enough money yet, or do we need to wait longer?"

Dad held up the blue envelope marked "Dino Land Savings." "Let's see how we're doing," he said. He emptied the envelope and counted the coins and bills with Mia. "We have $48 so far." The family's goal was $100.

They each suggested ideas for adding a bit more to the savings. Mom said, "If we make our lunches this week instead of ordering takeout, we can put the extra money in the Dino Land envelope." Mia added, "What if we play games at home Saturday instead of going to the movies? We could save money that way too." Lucas offered his piggy bank. "I can put in $1 from my allowance. I want to help!"

Dad nodded, "These are great ideas. Staying in for a movie or skipping takeout sometimes helps us reach our goal faster. And sharing from your allowance is teamwork, Lucas." Mom wrote their ideas on a notepad, along with everyday needs they must cover, like groceries and the electric bill.

The conversation turned to what the family needed that week. The fridge had a list with checkboxes for things like milk, bread, and fruit. Mia got a marker and helped check off foods they already had so they wouldn't buy what they didn't need. The family made a shopping list together, making sure to include items everyone liked but sticking to basics.

Dad pulled out an orange envelope. "This is for bills and groceries. The money must remain here to ensure that our lights stay on and we have food to eat. Lucas pointed at a treat he saw in a store flyer and asked, "Can we get ice cream, too?" Mom explained, "If we pay all the bills and still have some left, we can look for a special treat. But bills and saving for Dino Land come first." Mia suggested, "We could get a small ice cream tub instead of four cones. That costs less."

Everyone clapped for Mia's smart idea. They added the ice cream tub to the bottom of the list with a question mark. Dad taped the shopping list next to the savings chart—two columns, one for the money they needed, one for what they saved. Checking off each little victory became a mini celebration. Lucas even drew a dinosaur sticker every time the Dino Land envelope grew.

Then, something unexpected happened. The washing machine made a strange noise and stopped working during the week. Mom groaned, "Looks like we need to call a repair person." At the next family meeting, Dad explained, "The repair will cost $40. We need to figure out where we can adjust this week." The family took a deep breath and looked at the fridge chart.

Mia suggested, "Maybe we can wait on the ice cream treat just this once." Lucas said, "And I don't need new markers yet." Mom gave them both a gentle hug. "I love how you both help solve problems. It means we can fix the washer and still keep saving for our trip."

They shifted a bit of their money from treats and new art supplies into an envelope marked "Repairs." Dad wrote down the new plan. The family didn't get sad—they turned the washing machine fix into a game, pretending they were on a "money adventure" to save the day.

That weekend, after paying bills and fixing the washer, the family found they still had enough for a homemade pizza night. They used leftover veggies and dough from the last shopping trip. Before eating, Mia checked off "pizza party" on the chart, and Lucas added a smiley face beside the Dino Land column.

As everyone finished dinner, Mom said, "We made excellent choices together. Everyone helped, and now we're still on track for our adventure." Dad winked at Mia and Lucas. "When families talk and work together, we can handle surprises and still have fun."

After pizza, the kids thought of new questions: "How do bills work?" "How do you decide how much to save?" Mom invited them to draw their ideas for next time. The family meetings made talking about money feel friendly and open.

Kids can learn so much when they ask questions at home and share ideas with adults. There are additional methods to transform these conversations into games, drawings, or projects that make discussions about money enjoyable for everyone.

Money Talk and Drawing Activity

In the last section, readers saw a story about a family planning, saving, and working together with their money, showing how smart choices and teamwork help a family meet their needs and have fun. Every home has small habits and big traditions for managing money, and these things often make family life feel special. Even if families don't always talk about money, there are little hints in daily life grocery lists on the fridge, chats about which snack to buy, or a reminder that something needs to be saved up for. Learning how your own family handles these choices helps you see that managing money is not just a grown-up skill but something you can understand and practice, too.

Imagine being a reporter in your own home. Interviewing an adult about their financial usage allows you to gain insight into their inner workings. This isn't about getting the "right" answers. It's about discovering what works for your family, why your parents or guardians make certain choices, and how everyone's reasons might be a bit different. Sometimes, the best way to learn is by asking questions and really listening to the stories people tell.

Interviewing Your Grown-Up

Start by choosing one adult you feel comfortable talking with. This could be a parent, grandparent, older sibling, or anyone else who helps make money decisions in your home. Let them know you want to ask three questions about how they use money and that you're curious about what they do and why. Most adults are happy to explain, once they know you're honestly interested.

Here are some questions to get you started:

- What do you use money for every day?
- How do you decide what to save up for?
- What's something fun you bought with your money?
- Was there ever a time you had to choose between two things you wanted?
- Do you ever save money together as a family for a big goal?
- Can you tell me about a money mistake and what you learned from it?

Pick three questions you like. Start your interview by asking them one at a time. Listen carefully to each answer. Some people will tell stories, while others might give quick, practical replies. That's okay; everyone's style is a little different.

Drawing What You Learn

After your chat, try making a drawing to show what you discovered. For each question, draw a mini-scene or comic. Use color to show how the grown-up felt. Maybe your mom smiles as she puts coins in a jar marked "Vacation Fund." Maybe your grandpa frowns a little as he remembers spending too much on toys as a kid. Be creative. Add speech bubbles, doodle yourself in the corner listening or asking questions, or fill the page with details from the story you heard.

Here's an example:

Let's say you asked, "How do you decide what to buy at the store?" Your dad tells you, "I always make a shopping list, so I don't get things we don't need." In your drawing, you could show your dad picking out groceries, holding his shopping list, with little hearts around the snacks he loves most. Maybe you even draw yourself peeking over the cart.

Why This Activity Matters

Every adult balances needs and wants in a different way. By listening and drawing, you observe things such as how some individuals plan ahead while others adapt, or how everyone occasionally makes small mistakes. When you picture your grown-up contemplating saving, having fun, and making choices, you learn that money decisions are part of everyday life, not just big talks or lessons.

The act of drawing what you hear helps you remember the stories and tips. Colorful scenes stick in your mind much longer than just words. You also start feeling more confident asking questions and talking about money, which will help you as you grow up and start making your own choices.

Tips for the Interview and Drawing

- Use your favorite colors to show feelings and moods.
- Don't worry about making your art perfect—the goal is to capture the story.
- Add speech bubbles with the exact words your adult said.
- Include yourself in the drawings to show your part in the conversation.

Sharing and Reflecting

After you finish, think about what surprised you the most. Did the answers sound like what you expected? Was there anything new or amusing? If you want, share your drawings with someone else in the family. Talking about what you learned can lead to even more stories, advice, or good ideas about money.

Remember, adults aren't perfect and sometimes wish they'd made a different choice. That's part of learning, for everyone. By asking questions and using your creativity, you become a partner in your home's money story. Maybe next time your family talks about saving or shopping, you'll have a new idea to share or a question to ask.

When you reflect on your drawings and stories, you'll see that every family has their own way, and putting your ideas on paper helps you understand them more clearly. Keep your pictures to look back on as you grow, and notice how your feelings about money and decisions start to change, little by little.

Now that we've learned how grown-ups use money every day and how families work together to make smart choices, you can start to see that managing money is a team effort full of planning, saving, and sometimes saying "not right now" to remain ready for what matters most. By asking questions, listening to stories, and trying fun activities like drawing what you learn, you're already becoming a money detective in your own home. As you keep exploring how money works, you'll find even more ways to help your family, make good decisions, and reach exciting goals, all while having fun and learning along the way!

CHAPTER 9

OOPS! MONEY MISTAKES (AND HOW TO FIX THEM)

The moment Charlie realized his pockets were empty at the school book fair, his heart sank. Just days before, he had spent all his birthday money on shiny trading cards, feeling like the coolest kid around. But now, standing in front of that last copy of a coveted adventure book, he wished he had made different choices. It wasn't just Charlie; whether it's buying snacks too fast or trading away something important, everyone makes money mistakes, even grown-ups. What matters most is what happens next, how we learn, fix our slip-ups, and come back smarter than before. This chapter steps right into those oops moments and shows how they can lead to better money smarts and maybe even a few laughs along the way.

Everyone Makes Money Mistakes - Even Grown-Ups!

If you've ever wished you could hit an undo button on something you bought, you're not alone. Every person, even adults with years of experience, sometimes gets mixed up with money. Maybe you remember spending your allowance as soon as you got it and later wishing you'd waited for something even cooler. Or your friend traded two shiny stickers for a tiny rubber ball but then realized the ball wasn't as fun as it looked. Things like this happen to everyone. No one gets money right all the time, and that's perfectly okay.

Imagine an older brother who really wanted to win a stuffed bear at a fair, so he spent all his saved-up dollars on one game. He didn't win the bear, and now the money he'd been saving for months was gone. At first, he might have felt pretty upset or even embarrassed to talk about it. Another time, maybe you've seen a friend buy a toy that broke on the very first day, or you picked out a snack at the store and later wished you had chosen something different. Grown-ups have stories like this too. Sometimes parents might forget where they put some cash in the house or buy something on sale that turns out to be not so great after all. Mistakes with money don't have an age limit.

When things like this happen, it's easy to think you're the only one who's ever made a money mistake. Maybe your cheeks feel hot or your stomach flips a little. You might even feel like hiding what happened because you don't want anyone to know. But everyone messes up sometimes. Grown-ups have made some pretty silly money choices too. A lot of them even learned their most helpful tricks from slip-ups. Something honest happens when you talk about a mistake: it stops feeling so heavy, and sometimes you can even laugh about it. Sharing what went wrong is one of the strongest, smartest things you can do. Talking with a parent, teacher, or friend about a money mix-up can help you feel less alone and more ready to try again.

Let's say someone's birthday comes, and they get some money from their grandma. It's so fun to imagine all the things you could buy. One day at the store, there's a flashy toy on the shelf, and it looks amazing! The birthday money flies out of your pocket, and you walk home with the toy, only to realize that it's not as fun as it seemed or it breaks easily. That might be disappointing. But inside that disappointment is a secret message. The next time you have money, you might remember how fast it went last time and decide to wait before spending. Or maybe you'll ask more questions, check reviews with a grown-up, or save for something extra special that you know will last.

Mistakes are like clues on a treasure map. When something goes wrong, it's not a reason to be hard on yourself. Instead, it's a chance to figure out what to try differently next time. Every mistake gives you a chance to get better at money, just like learning to ride a bike means sometimes falling off. Over time, you start to spot patterns, like which items are worth your money and which trades make sense for you. Each slip-up teaches you a trick for the future.

It's totally normal to get upset or frustrated if your plans don't work out. Try to remember that these feelings mean you care about your choices and want to do well. Instead of being mad at yourself, ask, "What could I do differently?" or "What did I just learn?" Sometimes, talking it out makes things clearer. Maybe a friend has made a similar mistake, or maybe a parent has advice about what they did when they were your age. Sharing stories can even help everyone in your family or class get better at money decisions.

Mistakes aren't just about losing coins or making a trade you wish you could undo. They're also a sign you're trying, learning, and growing. Being curious about what happened turns little accidents into big discoveries. The more questions you ask and the more you talk about experiences, the smarter you become with money.

There are all sorts of ways money mistakes can pop up in your life. Sometimes it's spending all your cash at once. Other times, you might forget to keep track of your savings or trade away something special too quickly. But here's the best part: learning how to fix these mistakes and finding new ways to make better choices, is like unlocking a superpower. Soon you'll get to see what kinds of money mix-ups are common and learn easy ways to feel proud of your next step, no matter what happened last time.

What Should You Do When You Make a Money Mistake?

Have you ever felt excited about a new toy, only to realize later you spent all your money on something you didn't love as much as you thought? This happens to a lot of kids. Sometimes you might get a crisp ten-dollar bill for your birthday and plan to save it for something big like a science kit, but then you see a cool snack at the store and spend almost all of it right away. Maybe another time you bought something just because your friend had it, even though you didn't really want it that much. These are common money mistakes, and everyone, kids and adults alike, makes them.

One day, Amir got so eager to collect a set of shiny trading cards that he spent every single dollar of his allowance without even thinking. At first, it felt fun. But by the next week, when his friends started planning a trip to the ice cream shop, Amir remembered he had nothing left in his wallet. He felt pretty disappointed, but talking to his mom helped. She reminded him that lots of people get carried away and forget about saving for later. Mistakes like this show us what to do differently next time.

When you make a money mistake, start by taking a pause. Before spending, try to ask yourself, "Do I really want or need this, or am I just excited right now?" If you already made the mistake, like spending too quickly or forgetting to save, think honestly about what happened. It's not about feeling bad; it's about spotting what you learned.

Here are a few things you can do when you realize you made a money mistake:

- Stop and check how much money you have left in your wallet, jar, or piggy bank.
- Imagine something you wish you could still buy, but now you can't—what could you do differently next time?
- Talk to a parent, caregiver, or trusted adult. Ask for advice or even share your feelings about your mistake.
- Set a small saving goal, like putting just one dollar aside each week for something bigger or more meaningful.
- Before a big purchase, decide together with an adult if it's worth the money.

Some kids use three jars to help avoid money mistakes: one for saving, one for spending, and one for sharing or giving. The next time you get money from chores, birthdays, or a holiday, you could try putting a little bit in each jar. This way, you can protect some cash for big dreams while still enjoying small rewards.

Isa heard his class was taking a trip to the museum, and he wanted to buy a dinosaur figure from the gift shop. At first, Isa spent his weekly allowance on snacks at the school store, not thinking about the field trip. When the museum day finally came, he had only enough for a tiny button, not the dinosaur. Isa felt frustrated, but then he came up with a plan: he would draw a picture of the toy he wanted and save a few coins every week. Slowly, his jar filled up until the next special event came around, and this time he was ready.

Mistakes like Isa's can really help you get better with money. The important part isn't the mistake itself, but what you do after. Occasionally, the best ideas for saving money or making smarter choices come after a little slip-up. Later in this chapter, you'll read a humorous story about a money mistake that worked out perfectly, demonstrating how making mistakes can lead to new learning opportunities and creative problem-solving approaches.

Try out this self-help exercise the next time you think, "Oops, I messed up with my money!"

1. Think of a time you made a money mistake. Maybe you spent too soon, forgot what you were saving for, or traded for something that wasn't a good deal.
2. Write down or draw what happened. Did you buy chips before you meant to? Did you spend all your birthday cash on small toys?

3. Write or draw one way you could handle it better next time. For example, if you spent all your money and missed out on something better, you could plan to save half your next allowance.

Hana wanted a new sketchbook but kept using her money for candy and comic books. After missing out, she decided next time she'd ask her dad to help her set a saving goal: put $2 in her sketchbook jar every week. Soon enough, she got what she wanted and felt proud of sticking to her plan.

If you make a money mistake, remember you can always try a different plan next time. Mistakes are just steps along the way to being smarter, more confident, and happier with your money. And every single one, big or small, can help you come up with new ideas for reaching your goals.

Turning Mistakes Into Smart Moves - Stories and Activities

Charlie could hardly wait to tear open the shiny envelope stuffed with birthday money from his aunt. He'd been dreaming about this moment for days, already picturing himself at the toy store with swagger, snapping up anything he wanted. When he finally got to the cash register, his arms were full of trading card packs - dragons, space ninjas, and sparkly holograms, and he handed over every dollar with a proud grin. He left the store feeling like a champion.

That feeling only lasted until two days later at the school book fair, where every kid circled an epic choose-your-own-adventure book with a wiggling line at the checkout. It was the last copy, and when it was Charlie's turn, he reached into his pocket, and came up with nothing but lint and a sticky candy wrapper. He stood there, staring at the book, his excitement crumpling like a used napkin. That night, Charlie flopped onto his bed with a dramatic sigh and told his older sister about his "biggest-ever" mistake. She just grinned and said, "Hey, join the club I once spent ALL my allowance on pink glue and couldn't buy tickets to the water park. But there's always a way to fix things!"

He thought about the mountain of trading cards on his desk. The next morning, Charlie asked at the toy store if he could return a few unopened packs for store credit a tiny win! Then, at recess, he found friends who were looking for cards he didn't even want. One traded him a bookmark and some coins. With his little pile of money and new plan, Charlie marched back to the book fair just in time. He grabbed the book, paid, and this time had the best thing of all - a story to tell. Even though his mistake felt crummy for a while, it became a funny memory and a lesson he wouldn't forget: having a plan feels even better than a fistful of dragons.

Turning Mistakes Into Smart Moves

Mistakes with money happen to everyone even grown-ups. Maybe you get excited about buying something cool and forget you have other things to pay for, or you lend a friend some lunch money and then don't know how to ask for it back. Sometimes mistakes make you feel embarrassed, or wish you could hide under your bed until the feeling goes away. Here's the secret: every mistake is a clue to making stronger choices next time, and sometimes solving a problem can be fun or help you learn something new.

Instead of thinking, "Oh no! I messed up!" think, "What can I do with this?" You can practice this skill right now. Get some paper and pencils or markers. Here's what you're going to do:

A Money Mistake Comic

1. Think of a time you made a money mistake. If you haven't—or can't remember one—make up a story! It could be something like:

- Spent all your movie money on candy before the film, and you missed out on popcorn
- Bought snacks for friends but didn't have enough for the thing you really wanted
- Saved up for a toy, then realized you wanted something else but had no money left
- Gave your lunch money to a friend and felt weird asking them to pay back

2. Write a quick comic strip showing what happened. Here's how to get started:

- *Panel 1*: Show yourself with your money
- *Panel 2*: Show what you bought
- *Panel 3*: Show the moment you realize your mistake
- *Panel 4*: Show how you feel, maybe a sad face, maybe steam coming out of your ears!
- *Panel 5*: Draw yourself thinking of a way to make things better or asking someone for help

3. Now brainstorm at least two ways to fix it for next time. Use these questions:

- What could you do differently?
- How might you ask for help or make a new plan?

Here are some ideas:

- Promise yourself to save half your money before spending
- Ask a parent or friend for advice
- Team up with a sibling to buy something big and share
- Make a quick budget before spending
- Keep a small notebook to track what you spend

Get wild with your comic! Use funny faces, speech bubbles, or even superhero costumes. Mistakes aren't disasters; they're springboards for better ideas. Sharing your comic with someone you trust like a parent, friend, or teacher makes it even easier to feel good about bouncing back from mistakes. Sometimes just talking about it uncovers tricks you never thought of, and you might learn that everyone has their own money mishaps.

Learning from mistakes makes you clever with money in ways that just getting things right the first time never could. Every time you fix a problem or try a new idea, you get a little braver and wiser for next time. There are loads of other smart money moves, cool tips, and secret tricks waiting to be discovered, so get ready for even more adventures in mastering your money.

Now that we know everyone makes money mistakes, even grown-ups, it's clear that these slip-ups aren't something to be ashamed of, but chances to learn and grow. When you spot a mistake, you can pause, think about what happened, and come up with smart new plans for next time. Talking with someone you trust, saving little by little, or trying fun ideas like jars or comics can help turn tricky moments into superpowers that make your money choices better and stronger. So don't worry when things don't go perfectly - each mistake is just another step on the way to becoming a money whiz who feels confident and ready for whatever comes next!

CHAPTER 10
YOUR GOALS, YOUR FUTURE, YOUR MONEY!

Have you ever thought about something you really want to have or do someday? Maybe it's a cool toy, a fun trip, or even something bigger like saving up for college or a pet. How do you decide which wish is worth working toward? And once you pick your goal, what steps can you take to make it happen? Lots of kids wonder how to turn their dreams into real plans and how money fits into those plans. This chapter will help you explore how to choose your own personal money goals, figure out how to save for them, and start making your future exciting one small step at a time.

Dreaming Big and Small: Identifying Your Personal Goals

Imagine walking down the street and seeing a bright red bike with shiny wheels, just waiting in the store window. Maybe you pause and daydream about what it would be like to zoom down the sidewalk, wind in your hair, ringing the bell as you race your friends home. Or maybe you've watched videos of puppies tumbling over each other and you already picked out a name for the dog you hope to have someday. Each of these is a wish, a hope, or a dream, something you really want to happen. That's where goals come in. A goal is like a treasure map leading to something you want. Some maps are short, with the 'X' just a few steps away, while others take more time and patience to reach, but both are exciting to follow.

Let's think about the kinds of things you might want for your future. What pops into your mind when you imagine something special you'd save for? Maybe it's a set of art supplies to create new worlds on paper. Maybe you'd love to visit a water park or buy a new pair of soccer cleats for the big game. Some goals are even bigger, like planning for a family trip to another city, going to camp with your best friend, or one day saving up for college. Big dreams can feel far away and a little mysterious, like looking out over a mountain range and trying to guess what's on the other side. Small wishes are more like climbing a tree in your backyard, you can see the top, and it feels within reach, but you still have to find the best branch to grab next.

Both big and small goals are part of what makes life interesting. Saving up for a new comic book or snacks for movie night can be as satisfying as working toward a huge dream, because every goal helps you practice new skills. When you set your sights on something—even something you might hold in your hands soon, you start building habits that will help you with bigger challenges later. Little wins boost your confidence and show you what you can do when you put your mind to it.

Some goals are about things you want right now. Imagine making a list of cool toys, fun games, or tickets to a theme park. It's exciting to think about which one you want the most and how soon you could get it. Small goals can teach you how to wait and save, like waiting for a seed to sprout. You don't always have to choose just one goal, either. Your interests may change what sounds amazing today could be replaced by a new dream tomorrow. That's completely normal and part of growing up.

Big dreams are special, too. They teach patience and planning. If you want to get a pet, you might need to think about food, toys, and even doing chores to help out. If you picture yourself heading off to summer camp or starting college one day, that's a goal that unfolds little by little, with lots of steps on the way. Planning for something big can feel like building a tower with blocks; one piece at a time, stacking them higher and higher until, finally, you reach the top. Each step you take brings you closer.

Making a wish jar or a dream list is a fun way to start thinking about your own goals. Take a jar and some pieces of paper, and write down all your hopes: a science kit, a visit to the zoo, your first skateboard, or a puppy to cuddle. Each wish goes into the jar like a seed waiting to grow. You could draw pictures, make a poster for your wall, or talk with your family about your ideas. Sharing your dreams makes them feel even more real.

Ask yourself: If you could save for anything in the world, what would you pick? What makes you smile just to think about? You can talk to an adult, a friend, or a sibling to get more ideas or hear about other goals. Sometimes just chatting about what you want helps make the path ahead feel clearer and more fun.

Setting goals isn't just about buying stuff; it's about making your future exciting. Whether it's a little wish or a huge adventure, thinking ahead and planning makes big and small dreams possible. There's a thrill in watching your idea go from "just thinking" to "I'm making it happen." And it all starts with picking something you really care about.

Getting ready to choose your very first goal is where the journey begins. The next step is figuring out how to turn a wish into a goal and set a target you can actually reach, just like one kid who had a big idea and found a way to make it come true.

Setting and Achieving Money Goals: Learning from Real-Life Examples

Sophie had a big dream. For weeks, she had stared at the shiny red bike in the store window. The bell sparkled in the sun, and the tires looked ready for any adventure. Every time Sophie passed, she wished she could just ride away. But the bike had a price tag. She checked it one day - it cost $80. That seemed like a huge number.

Her parents told her, "If you really want it, you can save up. Let's figure out how." Sophie's mind was full of questions. Could she really do it? Where would she even start?

Sophie wrote "I want my red bike" on a bright sticky note and put it on her wall. This was her first step: picking just one wish. She thought about other things, like tickets to the roller-skate party or a fluffy kitten, but the bike topped her list.

When you choose one goal to focus on, it's much easier to make a plan.

Next, Sophie needed the exact amount of money. She double-checked the store tag. It was $80. Setting a clear, exact number made things less fuzzy in her head. Wouldn't it be challenging to save if you only said, "I want lots of money"? Specific numbers feel real. She wrote the number under her wish so she wouldn't forget.

Now she needed to figure out how to get the money. She sat with her family at the kitchen table and made a list. Her parents agreed to pay her $5 each week for extra chores, like sweeping the porch and watering the plants. She got $10 from her grandma for her birthday. She remembered coins in an old piggy bank. She asked her friend if she wanted help walking her dog, and her friend's mom said she'd pay for each walk.

Making a plan felt exciting. Sophie grabbed a notebook and drew a grid with boxes from 1 to 80. Every time she saved $1, she colored a box. Soon, she could see her savings growing step by step.

Stop and Reflect

- What is one thing you would love to save for?
- How much do you think it costs?
- What jobs or chores could help you earn the money?

A clear plan means less guesswork. Sophie figured out that with chores and some dog walking, she could reach $80 in about ten weeks if she saved every dollar. Some weeks, she got more; some weeks, less. If she felt sad about skipping ice cream, she looked at her chart and colored another box. She also put her prize money someplace safe, right in a big glass jar on her desk. When she counted her dollar bills and coins, she saw her hard work adding up bit by bit.

Sometimes she wanted a little treat, but she reminded herself, "This choice gets me closer to my bike." When saving felt tough, she asked her parents to cheer her on. Her brother suggested a lemonade stand for one last push. Sophie wrote her total down each week. It made her feel proud. Each colored box on her chart felt like a heartfelt hug.

Your Saving Steps

1. Pick one thing you really want. Write it down or draw a picture.
2. Find out exactly how much it costs. Check prices at the store or online.
3. Plan ways to earn and save, like doing chores, small jobs, or saving birthday money.
4. Track your progress using a chart, notebook, or jar. Mark every time you save a dollar.
5. Celebrate every small step, each dollar counts.

Example Chart

$ ♥	$ ♥	$ ♥	$ ♥	$ ♥	$ ♥	$ ♥	$ ♥	→	→	→	→	→	→	→	$	$	$	$	$	$	$

I have already saved these dollars   *I still need these dollars to go*

(8 dollars shown here as example) *(7 dollars still needed in the story)*

How to use it:

- • Every time you save $1, color or put a sticker on one empty box ▫
- • You can also draw hearts, stars, smileys – anything that makes you happy!
- • When the whole row is colored, you reached your goal!

Each square or symbol is a step closer. Color or mark your chart every time you add to your savings.

If you get stuck or feel like quitting, it's okay to ask for help. Maybe a parent, friend, or sibling can brainstorm ideas or even save with you.

At the end of eight weeks, Sophie's jar was almost full. Her chart was a rainbow of colors. She had saved $76 and still needed $4. It didn't matter that she wasn't finished yet. She felt stronger and more in control. Sophie grinned every time she looked at her jar and chart. She believed she would reach her goal.

In chapter 11, we will create colorful vision boards to help you picture and remember these goals every day. Until then, Sophie's red bike waited just a little longer, and her dream was nearly real. Maybe your wish can be, too.

Visualization in Action: Create Your Own Money Goals Vision Board

As you have taken the first jump by naming your real money goals and figuring out a plan to save for them, momentum begins to build. You've already met a kid who stuck to their plan and saw it pay off, turning an idea into a real-life reward. That energy gets even stronger when you turn your dreams into something you can see and touch, each and every day.

In the last section, you discovered how kids like you turn their ideas into exciting real-life goals, and found clever ways to save for something you really want. Now you'll take your biggest, brightest dreams and create something you can see every day making your vision even more real.

A vision board is a colorful poster, big piece of paper, or even a section of your wall where you collect drawings, magazine pictures, or photos of the things that feel important. These images stand for all the goals that make you excited to save. Imagine cutting out a picture from a magazine of a soccer ball if you want to join a team, or pasting in a photo of a puppy if you dream of saving for a pet. Some kids fill their vision boards with glitter, stickers, bright markers, and crafty borders. Along the way, you might add a drawing of a rollercoaster for a big day at the theme park, or a giant ice cream cone for your special treat. For one kid, every picture turns into a little reminder to keep going, to keep making smart choices. When your vision board hangs in your room, your goals stay in view and your imagination gets stronger, too.

Making your own Money Goals Vision Board feels like an art

day with a special purpose. Start by gathering your supplies. You'll need:

- A large sheet of paper, cardboard, or a poster board
- Markers, colored pencils, or crayons
- Old magazines or newspapers with colorful pictures
- Scissors and glue or tape
- Stickers, glitter, or washi tape (if you like)

Pick one or two goals that matter most to you, not just things you want, but things that make you feel excited inside. Search the magazines for pictures that match those dreams, or draw your own if there's nothing close. For example, maybe you cut out a picture of headphones for saving up for music lessons or draw your favorite snack for that day out with friends. If you want, write down how much each dream will cost right underneath the picture. Some kids like to put glitter around their biggest goal or use stickers to add personality. Others use neat labels, making sure every image has a place. Once you have all your images ready, glue or tape them onto your paper.

Right in the corner, make space for a progress tracker. Draw an empty jar or a tall thermometer and leave it blank. Every time you put money aside in your piggy bank or savings jar, fill in a part of your tracker. You'll love seeing how fast you're moving toward your dream. Your board is like a map showing where you want to go, and the tracker shows how far you've gotten on your adventure.

Hang your vision board somewhere you pass by every day. Above your desk, on your closet door, maybe right by your bed. That way, your goals become friendly reminders. It gets easier to say no to things you don't truly care about because your real dreams are in plain sight.

Looking at your vision board each day makes your goals stick in your mind. If you find yourself spending money on fleeting items, it can serve as a reminder to focus on the greater good. One child once drew a bright red bike and taped it next to a tracker. With each allowance, she colored in a section on her board. Day by day, the jar got full, and one afternoon she wheeled her new bike home, dream officially checked off.

Invite your family to join in, or ask a friend over to make boards together. Maybe your parent has a magazine with wonderful pictures of vacations, or your sibling wants to trade stickers. New dreams can always be added. As you grow, you can draw or paste more goals on the board. Some goals might change, and new ones will come to mind as you discover different things.

Your vision board is not just a list of hopes. It's a daily nudge that keeps you moving, helps you dream big, and reminds you to take small actions every day. With each goal you add or tracker you fill in, you get more ready for wise money choices and the next big adventure your future has in store.

Now that you know how to spot your dreams, set clear money goals, and make a step-by-step plan to save for them, you're ready to turn wishes into real accomplishments. Whether it's a shiny red bike like Sophie's or something special of your own, every small action you take brings you closer to what you want. You've learned that having a plan, tracking your progress, and keeping your goals in sight with tools like vision boards can make saving money fun and exciting. Keep dreaming big and small, stay patient, and remember each choice you make today is helping you build the skills and confidence to reach even bigger adventures tomorrow.

YOUR MONEY ADVENTURE STORY: SHARE IT HERE!

Sometimes, the best gift we can give is *sharing what we learned* so others can discover the same joy.

So here's a question for you: **If you could help another kid learn how to save money for their dream toy, game, or adventure, wouldn't that feel pretty awesome?**

Imagine a kid just like you picking up ***Financial Literacy for Kids***. They're curious, maybe even a little nervous about money, and they flip through the pages hoping to find something that makes sense. *Your review* could be the very thing that helps them say, "Yes! This is the book for me!"

That's why I'd love your help. Please leave an **honest review** of this book. Share your honest thoughts about what you enjoyed, what made you laugh, what provoked thought, or even what you'd like to see more of. Your words will guide other kids (and their parents!) who are seeking fun ways to learn about money.

When you leave a review, you're not just helping me as the author; you're helping future readers unlock *smart money skills* that can last a lifetime. It's like planting a money-tree seed that keeps growing for others.

Thank you so much for being part of this mission. And hey, if you know a friend, cousin, or classmate who wants to get smarter with money, share the book with them too. You might just become the hero of their money journey!

CONCLUSION

Wow! You've reached the end of this book, and that means you're officially a Money Master. Take a moment to pat yourself on the back; you've learned some amazing new skills that will help you not just now but as you grow up, too. Learning about money can sound tricky at first, but look how much you know already! From your very first dollar to smart saving, clever spending, giving to others, and even growing your money, every page has taught you something important. Are you ready to start using what you've learned? Let's bring it all together!

Think back to when you started reading. Maybe you were curious because you wanted to save for something special, like a video game, a cool backpack, or a gift for someone you love. Or maybe you just wanted to find out where money comes from and why adults never seem to have enough. No matter why you picked up this book, you've discovered one big secret: money isn't just for grown-ups. It's for you, too.

You've learned that there's more to money than just spending it as soon as you get it. You know how to earn your own cash, maybe by helping around the house, setting up a lemonade stand, walking dogs, or selling crafts. Earning your own money feels awesome, doesn't it? Every time you work hard and someone appreciates it enough to pay you, you can feel super proud. That's a skill adults use every single day, and you're already practicing it.

But what do you do with the money you earn? This is where your Save, Spend, and Share jars come in! Remember our fun game, where each jar has its own superpower? The Save jar helps your money grow bigger over time, the Spend jar lets you enjoy things right away, and the Share jar brings happiness to other people (and you). Each one is important, and now you know how to use them wisely.

Let's imagine you've just earned $10 for watering your neighbor's plants. What will you do? Maybe you put $4 in your Save jar, $3 in Spend so you can grab a treat or start saving for that skateboard, and $3 in Share to help buy school supplies for kids in need. When you split your money like this, you're practicing healthy habits that will last your whole life. Guess what? Not everyone learns this, even adults! That's what makes you a real Money Master.

Saving might have seemed hard before, especially when you want something right now. But you found out that waiting isn't just good, it can be fun! Watching your savings grow, dollar by dollar, is like watching your favorite video game score go up. And when you finally have enough to buy that thing you really want, it feels extra special because you made it happen.

Spending is fun, but now you know how to be smart about it. Remember when we talked about wants versus needs? Needs are things you truly can't do without, like food, clothes, or school supplies. Wants are things that are fun or make you happy, like toys or treats. Knowing the difference helps you make choices that won't leave you wishing you still had your money later. Smart spending means asking yourself questions before you buy: "Do I really need this?" or "Will I still want this next week?" If the answer is yes, then go ahead! You earned it.

Giving, or sharing, is something that makes you and the world better. Every time you share your money to help someone else, you become a superhero in their story. Your small gift can make a big difference. Maybe you donate to a charity, buy food for pets at the animal shelter, or help a friend who forgot their lunch. However you choose to share, your kindness shows you care and inspires others to do the same.

You also learned how money can actually grow. That's called investing, and it's like planting a magic seed. It takes a little time and patience, but someday it can turn into a big, strong tree. Even though you might not invest real money yet, you understand how it works and you're ready when the time comes. Some smart adults wish they'd known about growing money earlier, but you're already ahead of the game.

But guess what? Being a Money Master isn't just about what you do with your money. It's about teaching others too. Think of yourself as a money superhero. When your friends, brother, or sister want to learn about money, you can show them what you've learned. Teach them how to use Save, Spend, and Share jars. Tell them about earning money for jobs and how awesome it feels to save up for something big. Imagine if everyone you knew learned these skills just like you. The world would be full of smart savers, careful spenders, and generous givers, all thanks to you.

Maybe you'll have days when making good money choices feels tough. You might see something you want and feel like spending everything, or maybe you forget to put a little in your Save jar once in a while. Don't worry, that happens to everybody. Being a Money Master isn't about being perfect. It's about practicing, learning from mistakes, and keeping a positive attitude. Every choice is a chance to get better and better. If you ever feel stuck, talk with a parent, teacher, or another adult you trust. They might have some tips or stories to share too.

So, what should you do now? Here's your final Money Master Challenge: Go find your Save, Spend, and Share jars, or make some today if you haven't yet! Decorate them with stickers, drawings, or your favorite colors. Every time you earn money, divide it up between your jars. Challenge yourself to save for a goal, share with someone who needs help, and spend on something that brings you joy. Watch how much more fun and powerful money can be when you're in charge.

And remember, you don't have to do it alone. Share your Money Master skills with friends and family. Ask them what they do with their money, and tell them about your jars. See how you can help each other reach your goals, maybe by saving together for a group adventure or working as a team for a cause you care about. Money isn't just numbers or coins; it's something that connects us all.

The end of this book is really just the beginning of your adventure. Being a Money Master will help you in ways you haven't even thought of yet, from buying your dream bike, to surprising a friend, to making a difference in your community. Every dollar you earn, save, spend, or share is a step toward becoming the awesome person you're meant to be.

So take a deep breath, give yourself a big high-five, and get started. You're not only ready, you're unstoppable. The world needs smart, kind, creative Money Masters like you. Now go show everyone what you can do!

www.ingramcontent.com/pod-product-compliance
Lightning Source LLC
LaVergne TN
LVHW022228200926
848481LV00006B/2174